What's a Nice God like You Doing in a Place like This?

What's a Nice God like You Doing in a Place like This?

by
Wesley D. Tracy

Beacon Hill Press of Kansas City
Kansas City, Missouri

Copyright 1990
by Beacon Hill Press of Kansas City

ISBN: 083-411-3716

Printed in the
United States of America

Cover: Paul Franitza

10   9   8   7   6   5   4   3   2   1

A wise man once said that to know the affection of children is to know success. He was right. This book is affectionately dedicated to my three granddaughters, who have brought to me that kind of treasured success:

Melinda Michele,
Tracy Renee, and
Jennifer Marie.

They have taught me much about love, happiness, and hope.

Contents

Foreword

This is a book of intriguing sermons—the kind I like. I am confronted with a familiar Bible text. I say to myself, Oh, I know that story; he is going to pick up on this idea, or he could go that direction. After a few minutes I begin to think, Wait a minute; what's he doing with this text? Does he know what he's doing? And I am hooked, brought into running dialogue with the sermon, questioning, evaluating, listening, and thinking. What has happened is that the familiar story is no longer just an old friend; it has been re-created and interpreted from a fresh perspective and confronts me now as a new and challenging presence. A living word from God is heard, calling for new repentance, deeper commitment, and specific obedience. This is what God intended preaching should do.

Whatever forms our worship may take, whatever may be the most recent emphasis—atmosphere, fellowship, music, liturgy—the sermon is still at the center of what goes on in church. We still come to the house of God to worship Him and to hear something real from His Word. Many of the sermons we hear are reinforcement messages. That is, they reaffirm the things we already know, confirm the beliefs we already hold. Churchgoers tend to develop the bad habits of seeing what they expect to find when they read the Bible and hearing what they expect to hear when they listen to the sermon.

Wesley Tracy, editor of the *Herald of Holiness,* has given us a group of sermons that offer the biblical text a chance to speak to us differently from the way we ordinarily hear it. He demonstrates to us a fresh way of hearing the Scripture. He has chosen the kinds of texts we've always wanted to hear sermons on, but we never get what we expect. Instead, through some smiles, some tears, and always some surprises, we are confronted with new insight and fresh truth that probe us with judgment and heal us with saving grace. In vivid and expressive language he has brought great stories of our heritage into our current lives, enabling us to hear again the truth of God's audacious, tenacious, vulnerable love and commitment.

Don't start reading if you don't intend to read the whole sermon—or the whole book!

REUBEN R. WELCH
San Diego

Preface

Preaching is an event of the Word. The Living Word and the written Word, in conjunction with the spoken word, create an event of the Word, as the servant of the Word proclaims upon the housetops what he has heard in secret.

This definition of Christian preaching signals, among other things, that no sermon can ever be repeated. Preaching is an event, a historical happening involving interaction among the Spirit of Christ, the Bible, the preacher, and the hearers in a particular social setting. Therefore, the words of a sermon can be repeated, but the event cannot. Heraclitus was right—a man cannot step into the same river twice. Even if he comes back to the river before his socks dry, both the man and the river will have changed.

It is with an acute awareness of the unrepeatable that I cautiously offer this cluster of sermons for publication. The preaching events that have accompanied these messages in camp meetings, revivals, retreats, and Sunday services cannot be repeated in print, though deeply treasured, if not by the hearers, at least by the preacher. In the print media, we must settle for the mere words. Tides of feelings, facial expressions, tonal range, vocal pace, eye contact, significant pauses, response by auditors, and the like cannot be included. And, most importantly, nothing can be done to package and deliver the movement of the Spirit upon the hearts and wills of the preacher and the hearers. How prized are those experiences past when these sermons were used by the Spirit as the vehicle by which Christ walked once again among the people of His congregation, challenging, comforting, encouraging, rebuking, inspiring. No preacher controls the Spirit. No preacher knows when the Spirit will move upon His people, but he rejoices and trembles when He does. Anyone who has preached regularly for more than six months (six weeks?) knows that the Spirit, like the wind, "bloweth where it listeth" (John 3:8, KJV). A preacher soon marks as truth the statement made so long ago by Augustine that the preacher himself is merely "a little basket in which the bread is laid."

No sermon can be repeated. But the words of these sermons I do have; and if God chooses to bless them to the heart of some reader, then the chase to corral the words and hunt and peck them into my word processor will be more than adequately rewarded.

I want to point out to the reader a few things about this particular group of sermons. After 40 years of trying to preach—why these nine sermons? They seem to me to form a natural cluster. They are all about Bible characters, some famous, some hardly heard of. Further, they represent several variations within one homiletical genre. These sermons are more or less characterized by these four factors.

1. These sermons are fashioned in narrative style and inductive structure. I believe that the current human sensorium—our way of hearing, listening, thinking, and making meaning—is tuned to narrative style and inductive structure. Thus, almost any preacher's effectiveness can be enhanced by the use of story and the use of logic that flows from the specific case to the general principle (quite the opposite of the deductive logic of Aristotle in which most preachers have been trained). Of course, these sermons are not purely inductive. The addition of boldfaced subheads, an accommodation to the sight needs of the reader, conspire against inductivity. Further, purely inductive sermons are usually open-ended. The sermons in this collection begin inductively, but sooner or later a proclamation of the gospel, too narrow for open-endedness, appears. The primarily inductive structure and the narrative style, it is hoped, rescue these sermons from sounding preachy.

2. These sermons all hinge on a surprise to be found in the text or context. Markus Barth, the great New Testament scholar, urged preachers to "look for the surprise in the text." Not every text has a surprise to be found, but I believe that the texts used in this collection contain insightful surprises.

3. In these sermons, the historical, social, and cultural settings of the Bible texts are taken seriously. It is not

enough for today's preacher merely to know the Bible. He must also know something of the history, culture, and literature of the era and people that gave birth to the text. In this collection, such factors play an important part in the interpretation of the texts.

4. These sermons are basically biblical, one might even say basically Bible stories. That is, most of the preacher's time is spent in explaining, unraveling, and dramatizing the biblical story. This can be a high-risk venture in our culture, drunk on "relevance" and infected with the notion that anything older than last Tuesday is boring and archaic. The Bible, however, is much more relevant, modern, and interesting than most people think. I hope these sermons demonstrate that.

If there is any credit to be given for bringing a volume of sermons into print, it must go to my teachers—all of them. By that I mean those who have taught me formally and those who have taught me by their modeling, writing, and dialogue. I make no claim to precise originality—for what can I know that was not taught to me by someone else? Nevertheless, I regard these sermons as a gift from my teachers and my Lord, a gift that I pass along to anyone who cares to linger over these pages with an open heart and a spiritual ear pitched upward.

What's a Nice God like You Doing in a Place like This?

|||||||||||||||||||||||||||||||||||||||||||||

What's a Nice God like You Doing in a Place like This?

"Lord, all I've got to go on is Your word!"

After these things the word of the Lord came to Abram in a vision, "Fear not, Abram, I am your shield; your reward shall be very great." But Abram said, "O Lord God, what wilt thou give me, for I continue childless, and the heir of my house is Eliezer of Damascus?" And Abram said, "Behold, thou hast given me no offspring; and a slave born in my house will be my heir." And behold, the word of the Lord came to him, "This man shall not be your heir; your own son shall be your heir." And he brought him outside and said, "Look toward heaven, and number the stars, if you are able to number them." Then he said to him, "So shall your descendants be." And he believed the Lord; and he reckoned it to him as righteousness.

And he said to him, "I am the Lord who brought you from Ur of the Chaldeans, to give you this land to possess." But he said, "O Lord God, how am I to know that I shall possess it?" He said to him, "Bring me a heifer three years old, a she-goat three years old, a ram three years old, a turtledove, and a young pigeon." And he brought him all these, cut them in two, and laid each half over against the other; but he did not cut the birds in two. And when birds of prey came down upon the carcasses, Abram drove them away.

As the sun was going down, a deep sleep fell on Abram; and lo, a dread and great darkness fell upon him. . . .

When the sun had gone down and it was dark, behold, a smoking fire pot and a flaming torch passed between these pieces. On that day the Lord made a covenant with Abram, saying, "To your descendants I give this land" (Gen. 15:1-12, 17-18).

Now when Jesus was born in Bethlehem of Judea in the days of Herod the king, behold, wise men from the East came to Jerusalem, saying, "Where is he who has been born king of the Jews? For we have seen his star in the East, and have come to worship him." When Herod the king heard this, he was troubled, and all Jerusalem with him. . . .

When they had heard the king they went their way; and lo, the star which they had seen in the East went before them, till it came to rest over the place where the child was. When they saw the star, they rejoiced exceedingly with great joy; and going into the house they saw the child with Mary his mother, and they fell down and worshiped him. Then, opening their treasures, they offered him gifts, gold and frankincense and myrrh (Matt. 2:1-3, 9-11).

A Meditation for Epiphany

They are our spiritual ancestors in a special way. They were the first Gentiles to whom it was revealed that Jesus of Nazareth was the Son of God. I speak of course of the three wise men, who, in some symbolic way, represented the rest of us Gentiles at the crib of the infant Savior. It did not take God very long to announce *internationally* the coming of His own Son as Savior of the whole world.

Christians around the world celebrate the contribution of the wise men on the 12th day of Christmas—the first day of Epiphany. In various parts of the Christian world the first day of Epiphany or the first Sunday after Epiphany is called Three Kings Day.

Epiphany, generally defined, means a distinct divine revelation. The three wise men stood in our stead at the crib of the Christ child and shared firsthand in the greatest epiphany of all time. We do not know whether they found the Babe in the Bethlehem stable or caught up with Him later in a humble house, a basement apartment, a third floor walk-up, or a peasant's tent. But wherever they found Him, the place was plain, simply and obviously the dwelling of a poor family. Finding Him in such surroundings, I would not be surprised to discover that their first words were a gasp: "What's a nice God like You doing in a place like this?"

But before we explore that great epiphany further, I want us to consider an earlier one, a divine revelation that served as forerunner to the epiphany of the three kings. Consider the epiphany recorded in the 15th chapter of Genesis. It tells us something of the very nature of our great God. I did not understand it for a long time, but then my wife (who teaches the Bible as literature) explained it to me after I had shared my misunderstanding of it from the pulpit. "If you are going to preach on that passage, you ought to understand it first," she said. I listened to her and then went to check out her interpretation with three different Old Testament scholars. "Your wife is exactly right," they told me.

Abram's Call

After reading Genesis 15, I have come to the conclusion that Abram would have made a good Missourian. If some archaeological expedition digs up an ancient camel cart with a license plate that reads "SHOW ME," I will be sure that it belonged to Abram, that is, Abraham.

When God called Abraham (Genesis 12), He promised to make of Abraham and his children a great nation through whom all the nations of the earth would be blessed. What a wonderful promise, Abraham thought—but, after all, it's been a while, and all I've got to go on is a mere promise. Would God really come through? That was an important question because from the very beginning of his dealings with God Abraham's part was to be precise obedience. This was the very essence of all of Abraham's covenantal encounters with the Lord. God himself put it in unmistakable terms, "walk before me, and be thou perfect" (17:1, KJV).

Well, perfect walking is a tough business—who wants to put all that effort into perfect walking if God fails to keep His part of the bargain!

God understands, so we see Him in chapter 15 trying to reassure Abraham. God pledges to him, "Fear not, Abram, I am your shield; your reward shall be very great" (v. 1).

But for an old "show me" Missourian like Abraham, that was not enough. Abraham responded something like this. "Oh, yeah, that's easy for You to say. But just how is this *great nation* going to come about, since You have kept me childless all these years? Give me something to go on—show me!" You can understand Abraham's impatience. He was already of great-grandfather age and had not yet been a father. As for Sarah, she was no nubile youth herself.

So God decides to help Abraham with an object lesson. Maybe something concrete will batter this stubborn Missourian into faith and obedience. God ordered Abraham to go outside one night and look up (v. 5).

"What do you see, Abraham?"

"I see stars."

"OK, Abraham, count 'em."

"Huh? Why, I can't—I keep losing my place. There are too many; there must be millions of them."

"Just like the number of your descendants."

The object lesson seems to have helped for a while (v. 6), but then Abraham must have begun to think along these lines. Wait a minute. That was a neat object lesson. But there's a logical fallacy here. There is no syllogistic necessity between there being a lot of stars and me having a lot of kids. That's a logical non sequitur. "Listen, Lord, all I have to go on is Your word!"

So the Lord tries again. "I am the Lord who brought you from Ur of the Chaldeans, to give you this land to possess" (v. 7). Now Abraham has not only the promise of descendants but also the promise of a land, a country. Well, that's just a little too much for one man's faith. Listen to his reply (v. 8): "How am I to know that I shall possess it?" You can almost hear that Missouri twang in his voice: "Show me, show me, show me."

Of course, Abraham should have been worrying about the "perfect walking" he had been commanded to do. Instead he was all bent out of shape, staying awake nights, stewing and fussing about whether or not God was going to keep His part of the deal. God saw that Abraham was out of focus, worrying about the wrong things, and trying to mind God's business instead of his own. In fact, he seemed to be calling God into account with an attitude that sounded like, "Look, Lord, I've been doing my part; when am I going to see some action out of You?"

Therefore, out of mercy, love, consternation, or all of the above, God summoned Abraham to a contract signing, or a covenant cutting, as they called such transactions in those days (vv. 9-21).

The Covenant Cutting

God had promised, He had pledged, He had explained by way of object lessons. But to the unsure and uncertain Abraham, it was not quite enough. God, therefore, calls for something more drastic—a contract, a covenant. The contract signing to which God summons Abraham resembles the typical two-party suzerain treaty of ancient times. The two parties meet and discuss the terms of the contract, with each stating what he will pledge to do.

Since there were no word processors, few secretaries, and few contract makers who knew how to write, the signing of the contract was not done with one original and three Xerox copies. Instead they slaughtered an animal, chopped it in pieces, and arranged the pieces on the ground, usually with a path wide enough to walk on between the two halves of the animal. Then each party stated his part of the contract, and as he stated it, he walked between the pieces of the sacrificial animal. By walking between the pieces, he was saying to all who observed the covenant, "May I be hewn in pieces like this animal if I do not keep the pledge I make here today." If the two contracting parties were equals, they walked between the pieces together. If one was, for example, a ruler and the other a vassal, the one of low social rank went first. And God has called Abraham to just such a covenant cutting.

God orders Abraham to bring not one animal, which would have surely been sufficient, but five animals. This covenant will not merely be in triplicate, it will be fivefold! Following the command of the Lord, Abraham slaughters a heifer, a she-goat, a ram, a dove, and a pigeon. He halves the beasts, leaving the birds whole. He arranges them so that contract signers can walk between the pieces (vv. 9-10).

I am sure that as Abraham carried out these duties, he trembled and wavered. Could he really go through with it? Why had he whined, complained, and demanded a sign? This contract idea was not his notion. Why had he not let well enough alone? That "show me" attitude had gotten him into trouble again. He knew what he would have to pledge —he would have to vow that he and his descendants would walk before God and be perfect.

Frankly, Abraham did not know whether or not he could go through with it. But now he had no choice. The Lord of all the earth had subpoenaed him! How he must have trembled, contemplating walking between those halved animals certifying a covenant in blood, saying, "May I be hewn in pieces like these animals if I and my descendants fail to walk before God in perfect faith and obedience."

This was no time for glib promises, no time for flippant testimonies like we used to give on Wednesday nights: "I love the Lord with all my heart and want to go all the way with Him." No, this is serious business, and, frankly, Abraham probably wasn't up to it.

He prepared the sacrificial animals. But the Lord did not come. The carcasses did attract the vultures and the buzzards (v. 11). Abraham spent the day shooing the birds of prey off the holy sacrifice, and still God did not come. Would a God who had already put off His promises so long show up for such an affair? Maybe not. Maybe Abraham's religious imagination had run away with his wits—again. Why would God even care?

The Deity Arrives

But then at sundown, as the scripture says, at sundown, without understanding exactly how he knew it, Abraham is suddenly aware of the approaching Deity. God has come! The Lord of all the earth has arrived to conduct a solemn covenant. This will certainly not be a covenant between equals, which means that Abraham will have to go first. He will have to walk first between the pieces. But the Bible says that a trancelike terror of great darkness fell upon him. He was unable to move in the presence of the Holy One. He falls immobile to the ground; a stupor of great dread, a horror of great darkness overcomes him. Before the covenant-making God his knees turn to water, his demands melt away, his courage disappears like sand castles at high tide.

Abraham, it is time, time for you to make your pledge. But Abraham cannot move. In fear he looks toward those pieces of the sacrificial animals. He can hardly see them now, it is so dark. And what he sees is beyond belief, beyond imagination! God is here, all right, His presence signified by a smoking fire pot and a flaming torch, a double, unmistakable sign of His presence—a pillar of cloud and a pillar of fire, if you please.

And as Abraham watches in holy terror, the unimaginable happens. One of those symbols of God's very presence begins to move; slowly it passes between the pieces of the sacrificial animals—

Wait! Hold on here! This is backward! The vassal, the slave goes first! If Abraham could have found his voice, he might have cried out, "What's a nice God like You doing in a place like this?"

But he is too late. God has taken upon himself the role of a servant. He moves quietly between the pieces of the sacrifice, thereby proclaiming, "Abraham, may I be hewn in pieces like these animals if I do not keep my promises to you. Here, Abraham, I sign the covenant."

What a great story. No wonder it has been told for centuries around campfires, in desert tents, at village wells, in synagogues, and around dinner tables. It is a wonderful story of how Yahweh, the Sovereign Lord of the universe, took upon himself the role of a humble servant in order to reveal His steadfast love and redeeming purpose to our father, Abraham.

But let us go back to the covenant cutting. More surprises await us. This is, after all, a two-party treaty. Abraham, the Lord has taken the part of the servant, but you have not walked between the pieces to make your pledge. Poor Abraham! Seeing God take the role of a servant has not helped him overcome the terror of great darkness that has seized him. He still lies helpless on the ground in utter dread.

Abraham is unable to participate. He doesn't have what it takes. So, the Lord, by His action, says to Abraham, "That's all right, Abraham, I'll walk for you. I will walk in your place." And the other symbol of God's presence begins to move between the pieces. This is unheard of. It is incredible! This is condescension beyond comprehension!

In this two-party covenant, God is the Party of the first part—and God is the Party of the second part! Do you understand what is happening? It may be obscure to you, but Abraham was not missing a syllable. Notice that even in the brief account of this event found in Genesis 15, the Bible is careful to note that in this covenant God does all the walking; Abraham never walked at all.

Do you get the picture? As God takes Abraham's place and moves the second time between the pieces, He is pledging, "Abraham, may I be cut in pieces like these animals if *you* and *your descendants* do not walk before me in faith and obedience."

Wait a minute! This is too much. The Lord is saying to Abraham, "If you sin, I will suffer for it—" Wait a minute— what's a nice God like You doing in a place like this?

The Rest Is History

You know the rest of the story. The rest is history. Abraham's descendants forsook their Lord. They chased false gods, pursuing idolatry wholeheartedly. They even resorted to human sacrifice as part of the pagan religions they adopted. They gave themselves greedily to lust, drunkenness, oppression of the poor—and every sort of sin.

God sent warnings and blessings and judgments. He sent good kings like Hezekiah and Zedekiah. He sent prophets like Samuel, the praying prophet; and Elijah, the miracle-working prophet; and Hosea, the loving prophet; and Isaiah, the wise prophet; and Micah and Amos, the pulpit-pounding prophets; and Jeremiah, the weeping prophet. But nothing seemed to work. Abraham's children demonstrated for all the world to see that they would not, under any circumstances, keep the covenant. They proved they were bent on breaking it.

When every attempt at redemption had failed, and it was crystal clear that the covenant had been shattered, God came again in His Son, Jesus Christ.

Did you ever wonder what the Bible meant when it said, "But when the fulness of the time was come, God sent forth his Son" (Gal. 4:4, KJV). Perhaps it means that the fullness of time came when it became clear that the coveant would not be kept by Abraham's children. And God, true to the covenant, sent His Son in order to keep His word. On an evening long ago and far away He had pledged, "May I be hewn in pieces like these animals if *you* sin."

You know what happened. They made a crown of thorns and jammed it down on His head. They tied Him to a lictor's pillar and thrashed Him with a cat-o'-nine-tails, a whip with chunks of glass and rocks tied every few inches in each of its nine strands. The Romans (both Jews and Gentiles cooperated in the Crucifixion) hammered square-cut iron nails into His hands and His feet. They stabbed Him in the heart with a spear.

We gaze at Him on the Cross and understand Abraham's terror of great darkness. We note that "five bleeding wounds He bears," and we remember the five sacrificial animals—one wound for each of those animals. Somehow we now know that what those five different animals in the ancient Hebrew sacrificial system symbolized is fulfilled in this dear Savior hanging on the cursed tree. We cry out, "What's a nice God like You doing in a place like this?"

And He looks down from the Cross and says, "I promised. I promised that if you sinned, I would suffer for it in your place. I was serious on that covenant day so long ago and far away. You see, I love you—I love you this much."

Epiphany. We have looked at three of them today: the epiphany of God's covenant with Abraham; the epiphany of Christ's birth, the Incarnation; and the epiphany that occurred at the Crucifixion. We noted that the three kings who discovered the lowly circumstances of the Babe's birth probably felt like gasping, "What's a nice God like You doing in a place like this?" But we know now that they should not have been surprised. He took the role of a servant in His revelation to Abraham, He took the role of a helpless infant born in a donkey stall to poor parents, and He died on a cross like a despised criminal. All this He has done to teach us that salvation is by grace, grace freely offered to each of us. Perhaps we will have learned that lesson when we can encounter God in some lowly place and not say in slack-jawed surprise, "What's a nice God like You doing in a place like this?"

Come Running with a Bucket

"If only I had known you better . . ."

SCRIPTURE LESSON: *The book of the genealogy of Jesus Christ, the son of David, the son of Abraham. . . . So all the generations from Abraham to David were fourteen generations, and from David to the deportation to Babylon fourteen generations, and from the deportation to Babylon to the Christ fourteen generations. . . . and you shall call his name Jesus, for he will save his people from their sins* (Matt. 1:1, 17, 21).

What a boring way to start a book. No journalism teacher anywhere would give Matthew more than a C− on a lead like this. Some would write in the margins, "Where were you, Matthew, during the lecture on the narrative hook, that device whereby the writer snags the reader almost against his will?"

Doesn't Matthew know that genealogies—those dreary begat lists—are the most skipped passages by Bible readers? Even those ponderous Levitical codes, the "exciting" Book of Numbers, and the prophecy of Nahum are thumbed through more frequently by sleepy-eyed Bible readers than the begat lists. Does he think that we want to mess with any list of 42 generations?

But while a genealogy may be boring and eminently "skippable" to us, to the Jewish mind it is the natural place to begin. "Check out this fellow's pedigree," they would say. "Shake his family tree, and let's see what might fall out." The ancient Jews were as careful with their pedigrees as today's medical doctor who frames his diploma and hangs it on the wall in the waiting room for everyone to see. William Barclay observes that in Jesus' time a man lost his right to be called a Jew and a member of the people of God if his lineage showed the slightest admixture of foreign blood.

You could not become a priest, for example, by simply testifying with a tear-stained face that Yahweh had called you to the ministry. Oh no. The first thing the Levitical Ministerial Credentials Board demanded of the candidate was that he produce a pure pedigree that traced his unbroken lineage all the way back to Aaron, the granddaddy of the Hebrew priesthood. No pure pedigree, no priestly credential. Further, if any priest fell in love and wanted to get married (or if he wanted to get married for any other reason), he had to go before the Levitical Ministerial Credentials Board and present documents to prove that his fiancée had a pure Jewish pedigree for at least five generations. We see in the Book of Ezra, for example, dramatic stories of would-be priests dismissed from office because of polluted pedigrees.

The ambitious monarch, Herod the Great, being part Edomite, had the pedigree registers in Jerusalem destroyed so that no candidate for king could oust him on the basis of a purer pedigree.

To put all this in perspective, if we maintained this practice today, a preacher might be required to present a pure pedigree all the way back to Paul. His fiancée would have to produce a spotless genealogy back to John Wesley's time.

I have said all that to say this: It was of utmost importance who Jesus claimed to be. His genealogy was His credential statement. It was so important that the 42 generations of Jesus were listed in three sets of 14 so that they could be memorized easily. Memorized? Of course, in New Testament times a Jewish Christian would not have thought of witnessing to one of his countrymen without being able to recite Jesus' genealogy—would he? Had Campus Crusade existed then at Jerusalem University, it would have had to produce literature with five (not four) spiritual laws, and one of them would have been: "Jesus Christ is the Son of David and Abraham—and these 40 other folk."

A number of important truths are taught, implied, or

inferred in this credential statement of Jesus Christ. But I want to focus our attention on the one thing that I think is most remarkable, most marvelous, and even outrageous. Here it is—here in Jesus' very own credential statement, published right here in black and white for the whole world to see, five women appear: Tamar (v. 3), Rahab (v. 5), Ruth (v. 5), Bathsheba (v. 6), Mary (v. 16).

In those days nobody, I mean nobody, would dare put women in his official credential statement. Like Gentiles and slaves, they had no legal rights and no social status. The devout Jew, every day at the time of the morning prayer, lifted his bearded face toward heaven and thanked God that he was not a Gentile, a slave, or a woman.

Yet not only did Jesus claim five women, but He claimed four infamous women. We can perhaps understand His claiming the Virgin Mary, but who would claim kin to the other four? If you were to pick four women from Old Testament times, you would surely cite the four matriarchs cited in the Jewish Haggadah: "Four are the matriarchs, Three are the patriarchs, Two are the tablets of the law, And one is our God."

But in Jesus' credential statement, these honorable women are ignored in favor of some rather unsavory characters. What was Jesus thinking about? Doesn't He know we want a Messiah we can be proud of?

Let's take a closer look at the women in Jesus' genealogy. I should start with Tamar, since she is mentioned first, but I'm going to put her last and hope I run out of time and don't have to say much about her infamous exploits. I don't know how to talk about her claim to fame in polite company. So let's go on to someone more honorable:

Rahab, the Harlot of Jericho

You remember Rahab. The Israelite spies who were scouting out Jericho were almost caught in her place of business. Why would they, honorable men that they were, be there in the first place? The local authorities nearly caught them, but good old Rahab the harlot hid them under the "fodder," the Bible says. Can't you just see the screaming headlines in the *Jericho Times*—"Hebrew Spies Nabbed in Best Little Harlot House in Jericho!"

I know that some squeaky clean evangelicals have tried to promote Rahab from harlot to honorable innkeeper, but their efforts have been nearly fruitless in the face of the facts. Here's one reason why—the sign; remember the sign? When Rahab hid the spies, she made a quick deal. She said something like, "I know you guys are going to capture our city. If I hide you, will you please spare me and my family when the invasion occurs?"

But how, in the bloody confusion of war, could you possibly arrange to spare one household? The desperate spies told her to mark her house by hanging a red cord in her window! There you have it—the first red sign in a harlot's window! Some have tried to say that this red cord was some oblique, obscure symbol of redemption, but it is more likely that right here in this ancient event we see the origin of what today is called the red-light district. Can it be that right here in Jesus' genealogy is the mother of the red-light district? What was Jesus thinking about? Doesn't He know we want a Messiah we can be proud of?

Ruth the Moabitess

Ruth is mentioned in verse 5 of our text, Jesus' credential statement. Like Rahab, she is not even a Hebrew. But she is not just a Gentile—she is the worst possible sort of Gentile. She is a Moabitess. Do you remember the origins of the Moabites? You can read their squalid story in Genesis 19. There you will find the sordid story of a drunken father, Lot, in incestuous relationship with incontinent daughters and whelping a despised race—the Moabites. The foul origin gave the Jews spitting rights. On any sidewalk, on any street, in any shopping mall, on any path where a Jew met a Moabite, he would hiss through his teeth and spit in the direction of the despicable descendant of sensual sin.

The Moabites were so infamous that the Old Testament says they are not even to be allowed to come to church. In

Deut. 23:3, we find this law: "No . . . Moabite shall enter the assembly of the Lord; even to the tenth generation none belonging to them shall enter the assembly of the Lord forever."

What if we were still keeping that particular biblical law? It would mean, in terms of a rough comparison, that if back at the time when Columbus discovered America, one of your ancestors had been a Moabite, you would not have been permitted to enter this church today. Ruth, the very Ruth named in Jesus' credential statement, was a Moabitess.

In addition to being a member of that incestuous Moabite clan, there is the question of Ruth's own character. We know a few good things about her, but sometimes she was far from exemplary in character. For example, she wrote the book (with Naomi's help) on how to trap a husband. You may recall from your study of Old Testament times that the law in those days stated that any two unmarried people caught sharing the same blanket had to get married—whether anything immoral had happened or not.

Here goes Ruth after rich Boaz (one of two kinsmen with levirate marriage responsibilities to her). Boaz is tired and worn-out after working in the harvest fields all day. Still much grain remained to be harvested. Boaz and his crew did not even go home for the night. They camped in the fields in order to get to work at the crack of dawn, taking advantage of the cool morning air. About midnight, Ruth slips into the camp and lies down at the feet of the snoring Boaz and pulls his blanket over her. Sometime later, Boaz awakens and there's Ruth. Her coy grin in the moonlight seems to say, "Do you come quietly? Or do I cough, or maybe scream?" The wedding soon followed.

But Ruth, the despised Moabitess, the cunning trickster, is listed right here in Jesus' own credential statement. Outrageous indeed! What was Matthew thinking about? Doesn't he know we want a Messiah we can be proud of?

Bathsheba the Adulteress

Bathsheba baited David and then yielded to his sinful

seduction. And she did not seem to grieve too much when David murdered her husband, Uriah—after all, it's more fun to be a king's wife than a sergeant's wife. After a child had been conceived as a result of their lawless liaison, David arranged for poor Uriah to become a war casualty.

You remember the story. When Bathsheba turned up pregnant, David arranged for Uriah to have a military leave, a little R&R so that he could go home and spend some time with his wife. But poor old Uriah did not have a clue. He came back to the city, all right, but he would not go home to his wife. He made a big deal of it. He slept on the steps of the palace, saying, "Far be it for me to be at ease enjoying all the comforts of home while my comrades are dying in battle." David then had his men get Uriah drunk, but he still would not go home to his wife's bed.

He was then sent back into the battle, bearing his own death warrant. At David's order he was put at the front of the battle where he was sure to lose his life. He was chopped down, and Bathsheba seemed to be as happy as a canary-snapping cat about the whole thing. Surely she did not out-sin David in this affair, but in all the sources I have been able to find in the Bible and in the ancient Hebrew writings, I have not found one author who said one good word about Bathsheba's character. But here she is, listed in Jesus' own credential statement. How could Jesus claim such a woman? Doesn't He know we want a Messiah we can be proud of?

Tamar, the Cunning

I'm glad I am about out of time. What can you say about Tamar's nefarious escapades? She had a husband named Er, but he died—"The Lord slew him," the Bible says (Gen. 38:7). Tamar took Er's brother Onan for her husband, but because of onanism, the Lord slew him too. Next Tamar tried to get a man named Shelah for her husband, but she was denied this man. Not many women here today would want a husband named Shelah, but Tamar did.

What was she to do? Though her plan included poetic justice and some primitive cunning and even a crude sort of honor, we must today file her story under "despicable." To make a long and awkward story short, she resorted to harlotry, seducing her father-in-law in an attempt to solve her family and economic problems. And, unlike Paul Harvey, I'm not going to tell you "the rest of the story." Read about it in Genesis 38. In fact, there is only one reason that I mentioned her at all. That's because in His own credential statement, Jesus claims her as ancestress.

There you have them: Tamar, Ruth, Bathsheba, and Rahab. If you had sifted through all the centuries of Old Testament history, you could not find four persons more unlikely to ever appear in the Savior's credential statement. But Jesus claimed them all—right out front, in public for all the world to see. What was He thinking of? Doesn't He know we want a Messiah we can be proud of?

So What?

That brings us to the "so what?" part of the sermon—every sermon should have one. What is Jesus saying to us? For one thing, He is saying that with the in-breaking of the kingdom of God upon history, some old barriers are coming down:

1. The barrier between *male and female* is coming down. By including five women in His genealogy, He announces that women are just as precious in His sight as any man ever was—and that both men and women are equally important to His purposes. This may seem insignificant to you, but in those days it was indeed "news." In some corners of our modern world this "good news" is still needed.

2. Second, Jesus is saying that the barrier between *Jew and Gentile* is coming down. By citing a Moabite, a Canaanite, and the wife of a Hittite, Jesus declares that it doesn't make any difference what kind of an "ite" you are. Divine favor, salvation, really is by *grace,* not race.

3. Third, the barrier between *saint and sinner* is coming down. This is an announcement that neither the blatant lawbreaker nor the self-righteous law keeper can find salvation except by grace and grace alone. The old idea that a code-

keeping legalist can earn his salvation by being better than other sinners perishes forever.

What Does This Mean to Me?

1. First, it means that my race or nationality is no plus or minus as far as God is concerned. In God's sight, my being a white Anglo-Saxon gives me not one hint of an advantage over the simplest person in the most primitive jungle in the world. But my race gives me no disadvantage in comparison to any other son or daughter of Adam or Abraham.

2. It means that my gender is no testimony to my personal and eternal worth.

3. It also means that my past failures and sins need not be final, and that my past self-righteous strivings cannot buy my salvation.

But those statements are so abstract and general that you may not catch their significance. Therefore, I want to reduce this whole sermon to one truth you can tuck into your heart and live by. If you can internalize this, it will change your life forever! It comes down to this: Since Jesus claimed as His own these four sinfully notorious women— not on the sly, but right out in public for all the world to see, *there is absolutely no reason to think that He will reject you!* Let me say that again. *Since Jesus accepted them, there is absolutely no reason to think that He will reject you!*

But you don't know how rotten I've been, you say. My reply is, If Jesus claims a Moabite from a wretched, incestuous clan; if He claims Rahab of red-light fame; if He claims Bathsheba, the heartless adulteress; and if He claims Tamar, is there any shred of evidence that He will reject you? No! No—a thousand times, No!

Jesus assures you through His preaching, His teaching, His examples, His words, and even through His genealogy that He will accept you just as you are.

Many of you even at this moment are separated from God by the guilt of sin. The devil, disguised as your guilt complex, tries to tell you that you are so bad that you will never be accepted. But the devil is a liar. Jesus is telling us by

His very own credential statement that if He accepts people like Rahab, Ruth, Bathsheba, and Tamar, He will accept you, even you—me, even me.

Nancy Spiegelberg celebrated her discovery of this truth with these words.

> *Lord,*
> > *I crawled*
> > *across the barrenness*
> > > *to You*
> > > *with my empty cup*
> > *uncertain*
> > > *in asking*
> > > > *any small drop*
> > > > *of refreshment.*
> *If only*
> > *I had known You*
> > *better;*
> *I'd have come*
> *running*
> *with a bucket.**

Jesus will accept you just as you are. Come running with a bucket. Do not make the mistake of the self-righteous. They say I cannot come now. One day, when I get my life in order, I will come. But that is works righteousness, which will never "work." We must come to Him just as we are—with all the sins of all the past weighing us down. Jesus Christ accepts sinners; He died only for sinners.

There is no doubt that He will accept you. Come running with a bucket. His grace is abundant. He will accept you just as you are, but He will not leave you just as you are. He will liberate you from the guilt of all the sins of all the past. He will forgive you, love you, and redeem you from the guilt and power of sin. He will set you free. His grace overflows; come running with a bucket.

*Used by permission of the author.

A Boy Named Disgrace

"Could a nameless nobody born on the wrong side of the tracks in the shadow of shame have any excuse to hope?"

SCRIPTURE LESSON: *And Jabez was more honourable than his brethren: and his mother called his name Jabez, saying, Because I bare him with sorrow.*

And Jabez called on the God of Israel, saying, Oh that thou wouldest bless me indeed, and enlarge my coast, and that thine hand might be with me, and that thou wouldest keep me from evil, that it may not grieve me! And God granted him that which he requested (1 Chron. 4:9-10, KJV).

"It's a boy, a fine, healthy baby boy," the midwife announced to the exhausted mother. "Congratulations; you are the mother of another son." But the mother did not even smile; she was quietly weeping.

A little later they brought the newborn son, carefully wrapped in a blanket, to her bedside. Her husband, her other children, and some other relatives gathered around her bed. They wanted to be there for the naming ceremony. In those ancient times it was the mother's privilege to name the children (v. 9).

"Well, let's hear it," they chimed. Usually the naming ceremony was as happy as a birthday party. But the woman holding her new son looked grim. An uncomfortable silence filled the room like a fog. Then she spoke:

"His name is Jabez."

"What?"

Bitterly she repeated, "His name is Jabez."

"Why would you name an innocent child Jabez?"

"Because," she snapped, "I bore him with sorrow [v. 9].

I'm sorry he was ever born. I'm doubly sorry that he was born into this wretched family."

So, enter Jabez. Another in the long parade of the world's unwanted, unloved children. And his name told the world what he would have liked to keep secret. The name Jabez comes from a root word whose derivations are translated: *Great Pain, Super Sorrow, Grief, Doomsday, Hopeless.* Herbert Lockyer says, however, that the best translation of Jabez is *Disgrace.*

The Family History of Jabez

It must have been quite a chore to grow up with a name like Disgrace. How would you feel on the first day of kindergarten when at "show and tell" time you were introduced as Disgrace? I imagine, too, that if you were playing baseball with the other boys in the neighborhood, and suppertime sneaked up on you, and your mother went out in the street and began to scream, "Disgrace," you went running home as fast as you could, even if it was your turn to bat.

How could you ever explain a name like Disgrace without having to try to explain away the disgrace that had fallen upon your family? The disgrace was real, and Jabez' mother had felt it so deeply that she named her boy after it. Disgrace and shame hung in the air like soot around the house of Jabez. To make matters worse, Jabez' father and big brothers were living up to the family's bad reputation.

The vices of these men had caused them to lose the family inheritance. Remember that when the children of Israel had conquered the Promised Land, each family was given 40 acres and a mule—or some such grant. But Jabez' family had lost its inheritance. Apparently, they lost it through the drunkenness of the father and the older sons.

Their disgrace was so strong that they lost their land, and their family name was dropped from the ancient real estate logs and from the official genealogies. That's the way the ancient Hebrews handled disgrace—they pruned you off the family tree. If one or two or three generations were an embarrassment, they just omitted them from the family tree, and there was no record that they even existed. That's why it is so hard to date anything from the ancient Hebrew genealogies. Any genealogy may simply be a list of the honorable, or at least famous. The family of Jabez lost its inheritance, and the family name was scratched from the roster of the honorable.

Some of the Jewish people still practice such measures. A Jewish man named Bennie was saved at the church I attend. He wrote home to his family in New York and told them that after all these years he had found the Messiah—Jesus. A few days later he got a trunk in the mail, a big trunk. In it was every gift and every photograph he had ever sent home to his family. There was a note that said, "As far as we are concerned, you are dead. We have had your funeral. You have disgraced us." That is the kind of pressure that Jabez' mother was feeling when she named her son Disgrace.

Jabez Goes to Prayer

I think you could say that Jabez had three strikes against him when he was born. We cannot expect much from a kid named Disgrace, an unloved, unwanted child, born to an alcoholic father, and raised on the wrong side of the tracks. It is true that the dark shadows of the past shrouded Jabez' prospects. But Jabez did one thing right—he prayed about his state of affairs.

His prayer is recorded in the briefest sort of summary in our text. Look at his prayer.

"Oh that thou wouldest bless me indeed" (v. 10). The sense of the prayer in modern English is "O Lord, bless me, even me." His prayer was properly humble. "Bless me, O Lord, even me, a boy named Disgrace, a poor kid from the wrong part of town." His prayer was humble, and not at all in the spirit of a paperweight placard I saw on an executive's desk that read, "I am superior and couldn't be prouder, and if you cannot hear me, I'll yell." No, Jabez came humbly to God. And, although he of all people might have done so, he did not make his prayer an excuse-ridden protest against Providence or society.

The second part of his prayer as it is outlined here is *"enlarge my coast."* This was a prayer for economic prosperity. More specifically, he was praying that the Lord would restore to him the farm that his family had lost. It is quite likely that Jabez' family had become debt slaves and now lived in one corner of the land that had once been theirs. The mortgage holder probably lived in the main house, and they were relegated to the hired hands' shack. Jabez prayed, "O Lord, restore to me my family's inheritance. Give me back the family farm."

Note that ambition and religion are not automatically incompatible. When God redeemed Paul, He did not make of him a shriveled-up little cabbage. Rather God rechanneled his compulsive nature, and he achieved great things in the name and in the power of God. It is acceptable for a Christian not only to *be good* but also to *do good* and to *make good.*

Victor Hugo wrote that, "Ignominy thirsts for respect." It was so with Jabez. He prayed, *"enlarge my coast."*

Note the next phrase of this prayer, *"and that thine hand might be with me."* This is a prayer for divine guidance and protection. Unlike the New Age movement, Jabez had no illusions of self-sufficiency. He knew he could not make it without God's help.

He also prayed, *"that thou wouldest keep me from evil, that it may not grieve me!"* In all probability Jabez was praying for deliverance from the specific evil that had destroyed his father and brothers and disgraced his family—drunkenness. And this was a real danger. How many sons of alcoholics themselves become alcoholics? How prone we are to repeat our parents' own parenting mistakes—even when we know better.

Jabez grew up watching his father and brothers cope with life's problems by turning to drink. Doubtless, it would have been easy to have followed them down that disgraceful trail to ruin. But as he felt that downward pull, he prayed in desperation that he would not fall into that numb, senseless oblivion of drunkenness.

The scholars who know more about Hebrew than I,

say that in this last phrase of the prayer there is a play on words that does not come through in English. "Keep me from evil, that it may not grieve me!" means, "Let not Disgrace be disgraced." So Jabez wings a heartfelt prayer heavenward that God will help him not to live up to his name— "Let not Disgrace be disgraced." He called upon God because he wanted to be better than his label.

Surely Jabez spent many agonizing hours in prayer. Verse 10 is only a skimpy summary of his prayer life. Writing was a slow and painstaking process in those days, and writing materials scarce. Therefore, most written things were mere summaries. Most of the Old Testament is written this way. The author of the Books of Chronicles was an astute summarizer. He closes the two-verse story of Jabez with, "And God granted him that which he requested." "Whoa! Hold on here," we would say to him. You are skipping the best part. It is almost as if the chronicler figured that anybody reading this would already know the famous story of Jabez and could fill in the details from memory. He seems to be saying here in verse 10, "And as you all know, God granted him that which he requested." The problem for us modern readers is that we are in the dark about this man's story. Only three verses in the Bible mention him at all.

We do know that after he prayed the prayer we have been studying, he became a God-fearing, clean-living, self-disciplined man. Besides our text, the only other Bible reference to Jabez connects him with the Rechabites. It seems that Jabez either joined or helped found that religious organization, the Rechabites. But why would Jabez want to be involved with the Rechabites? Because of their one dominating rule of life. Remember what that was: no booze, no drinking, no liquor, no alcohol, not even rum cake at Christmas!

Since young Jabez went straight out and joined the Alcoholics Anonymous of his day, it is probable that drink was what dragged his family into the gutter. Note that when Jabez got serious about turning his life around, he joined a church, or at least a religious organization that met his needs. Note also that he was drawn to a group that really stood for something.

God Answers the Prayer of Jabez

What would God do with the prayer of this unwanted child from the wrong side of the tracks, with Disgrace for a name? Well, the Bible says that God granted him what he requested. We know then that he was delivered from the evil of drink. And we know that he got his "coast enlarged." That is to say that he got the family farm back. The Bible tells us that, at least indirectly. But the choicest details of Jabez' story are not included in the Bible. We can learn much more about him, however. One source is the *Chaldee Manuscript*. When the Jews were hauled off into Babylonian exile, they decided to write down their history just in case they never got back home to establish their nation again. In this history they say quite a bit about this man Jabez.

We discover that he had quite a hand in Hebrew history. He got not only his farm back but much more. For example, it seems that Caleb made a swaggering brag to Joshua that, even though he was now 85 years old, he was just as strong as he was when he was 40. He went on to promise Joshua that he could whip those giants in the mountains of Kerjathsepher who were keeping them out of one big chunk of the Promised Land. Joshua commissioned the old man to do it rather than just talk about it.

The truth is that Caleb wasn't up to it. But he figured out a way to have it done. He threw a big feast and invited all the strong young men he could find to come. Caleb's beautiful daughter Achsah was the hostess for the banquet. I doubt that she showed up in jeans, tennie runners, and a T-shirt with a rock group's name or some other absurdity painted on it. I doubt that she had her hair up in curlers or slouched around the room to the vibes of a Sony Walkman. No, this was an event too important for all that.

After dinner, Caleb got up to make a speech. To the young men around the table he must have said something like, "I have invited you here tonight because I want to give my daughter Achsah to one of you for a wife. I know you are all interested, because you have been watching her more than the roast lamb I served."

Doubtless this announcement brought a cheer. But Caleb went on. "I promised Joshua, our leader, that I would conquer the giants of Kerjathsepher. But I am an old man. I can no longer lead a troop in the field. Therefore, I will offer Achsah as bride to any one of you who will drive the giants out."

The young stalwarts had to think this over. The feast was fine, and the thought of marrying Achsah brought tingles of delight, but fighting giants was another matter. One man quickly stood, however, and accepted the challenge—Jabez.

Jabez organized a troop, marched on Kerjathsepher, whipped the giants, and returned and married Achsah. Wow, God is answering prayer. Jabez got his farm back, whipped the giants, and married a beautiful wife.

But Achsah was more than beautiful—she was rather wealthy. When Caleb asked her what she and her bridegroom, Disgrace, wanted for a wedding present, she said she wanted the ranch at Hebron, the one with the two springs on it. Two springs! A two-spring ranch in arid Palestine! Oh, my! That's like asking for the Hilton Hotel as a gift! That was a lot more than the pen and pencil set that Caleb had planned to give them. But in the end, he came through. He gave the two-spring ranch to Achsah and Jabez. I can see it now—117 degrees in Palestine. The whole country is sweltering. But there are Jabez and Achsah under a big beach umbrella, sipping Dr. Peppers, with their feet in the springs.

Jabez prayed to get his farm back, but God had even more in mind. He got his farm back, a beautiful bride, and a beautiful ranch with two springs. Not too bad for a kid named Disgrace, born in poverty with three strikes against him.

He asked for a little, and God had given him more than he dared hope for, and certainly more than he deserved. But God wasn't through blessing Jabez. Soon we find that Jabez has a town named after him. In 1 Chron. 2:55 we find a reference to it. Not bad for a kid who had nothing. God gave him victory over alcohol, victory over the giants, gave his farm back, gave him a beautiful bride with a ranch and two springs—and now a town, which he probably founded. And this is not an ordinary town. It's not one of these one-stoplight towns filled with weedy lumberyards and abandoned gas stations. No, sir, this is a college town. The Bible says, "The families . . . of the scribes . . . dwelt at Jabez." The scribes were the theological students of the day, an absolutely necessary religious order. They were the people who copied the Scripture, memorized the Scripture, read and interpreted the Scripture to the whole nation. They lived and studied in Jabez. They prepared for ministry in the school that Jabez himself founded. Could this be the first Bible college ever founded?

God just pours on the blessings. Poor old Jabez. He had nothing, born on the wrong side of the tracks, unwanted, named Disgrace, but he prayed and disciplined himself, and now we see he got his farm back, a bride, a two-spring ranch, a town, and a theological college! Not bad for a kid named Disgrace.

The *Chaldee Manuscript* describes the school Jabez founded. It names four characteristics of the students in Jabez' school. You could guess the first, couldn't you? Don't you know that in any school founded by Jabez there would be a lot of prayer majors? Sure enough, the *Chaldee Manuscript* declares that they "prayed persistently." Second, it says that they "worshiped fervently." I'm not exactly sure what that means, but it suggests that when they worshiped, corporately or privately, they meant business. They took the worship of God seriously. Third, this document says that they "sang with trumpetlike voices." Last, it says that the students in Jabez' school "preached with a spirit of prophecy." That's not too bad for a kid named Disgrace, who had three strikes against him. He got his farm back, whipped the giants, married a lovely bride, got a two-spring ranch, a town, and a school full of students who prayed persistently, worshiped fervently, sang with trumpetlike voices, and preached prophetically.

It seems as if Jabez could just rest on his laurels and sit back and take life easy. But God is not through with our boy named Disgrace. According to the *Chaldee Manuscript*, God called Jabez himself into the ministry. So, president and founder, Jabez enrolls in his own school as a freshman, studies hard, and finally gets his Ph.D. in Old Testament. He became a doctor of the law, a professor in his own school, teaching the younger generation what God can do—even for kids who start out in poverty with three strikes against them. What a blessed journey of faith for Jabez, from that sorrowful day when he was born, to his position now as professor of Old Testament.

But God has a bonus system that just keeps on pouring out blessings. You guessed it—God had even more in store for Disgrace. He was elected president of the land. They called it judge then. During his tenure in office (40 years, probably a euphemism for a good long time) he led the people in a revival of religion and restored, according to the *Chaldee Manuscript*, 1,700 traditions of Moses. He also whipped two enemy kings while he was at it.

And then comes what is probably the greatest event in the life of Jabez. Here's Jabez—named Disgrace, unwanted, got his farm back, got the girl, got the two-spring ranch, got the town, got the school, got his Ph.D., and then got elected president. But the best was yet to come. His loyal subjects gathered before him one day. They said to him, "We do not like your name. We believe you have been misnamed. We want to change your name from Disgrace to Othniel." And so his name was changed from Disgrace to Othniel, which means "Lion of God"! In Old Testament times, a name was meant to designate one's character. For Jabez, Disgrace no longer fit. God had changed his character and his name. God is in that business, you know, the business of giving a new name to those who seek His face.

Epilogue

Jabez prayed for a little and got a lot. Prayed for the farm back and got all that long list of bonuses I have been reciting to you. He also got a religious organization that out-lived him. You remember that he was associated with or helped to found the religious order called the Rechabites. Hundreds of years later, when God is trying to get Judah to repent rather than go into captivity, we hear from Jabez' spiritual descendants again. God inspired Jeremiah to plan a rally day, a Sunday School contest or something. God directed him to invite some special mystery guests.

Everyone came to church to see what would happen. The special guests included Jaazaniah, the chief of the Rechabites, and other Rechabite leaders (read about this in Jeremiah 35). Jeremiah invited them up to the front and presented them a special gift. He offered them jugs of wine and cups enough for them all so that they could all drink. "Drink some wine" (v. 5, NIV), Jeremiah urged. This made the Rechabites furious. "We will drink no wine," they declared. "For Jonadab the son of Rechab our father commanded us, saying, Ye shall drink no wine, neither ye, nor your sons for ever" (v. 6, KJV).

Then Jeremiah stepped up before their outrage got out of hand and told them that he knew they would keep their vows to God. Then, turning to the congregation of the people, he blessed the house of Rechab (Jabez' old outfit) and in so many words told the people that if they had been half as serious about keeping their vows to God as the Rechabites had, God would spare them the destruction and captivity that was sure to follow if they did not repent. Jabez' influence was still living then.

And it was still living in New Testament times. Eusebius records in his *Ecclesiastical Histories* the final sermon of James, the brother of Jesus. James was burdened for the salvation of Israel. And while Peter and Paul were conquering the Gentile world for Christ, James ministered in Jerusalem. He prayed in the Temple for the salvation of Israel so long and so often that they said his knees were calloused like camels' knees.

Several years had passed since Jesus had been crucified and raised from the dead. The Passover festivals loomed before the Jewish leaders in Jerusalem. They expected Jews from all over the world to crowd the streets of the city. Among them would be many evangelistic Christians. There would be tension, maybe even riots. The Christians were so hard to control. The peak tourism season could be ruined. The chief priests went to James the Just, as he was known, and asked him to speak during the Passover celebrations. They said that they appreciated his moderate way of being a Christian. He prayed and prayed, but he didn't cause trouble. We want you to quiet the crowds during Passover. After all, some of these Christians are fanatics. Tell them not to overdo this Christian business. We don't need any riots, or Hallelujah services, or evangelism that violates good taste. James accepted.

They put him up on the pinnacle of the Temple—a 30-foot-high pulpit above the crowded courtyard. They introduced him, and James began to preach. And preach he did. He proclaimed Jesus Christ as the only hope for salvation, both for Jews and Gentiles. The high priests shouted, "Ho, ho, even the just one has gone astray!" Scrambling up the scaffolding, they seized James and threw him out of that 30-foot pulpit onto the cobblestones below. As he writhed in pain, they began to stone him. James began to pray his Brother's prayer, "Father, forgive them; for they know not what they do" (Luke 23:34). Only one person came to his defense. A man from Jabez' old outfit, a Rechabite priest, rushed up and tried to shield James. He cried out, "Stop! Do you not hear that the just one is praying for you?" But even as he spoke, an angry man pushed past him and smashed the skull of our Lord's brother, James, with a fuller's stick, a baseball-bat-sized club that the soap makers used. It was a tragic event. But right in the middle of it was one of Jabez' spiritual descendants trying to do right. So Jabez' influence lived on. What better use of life than to spend it for something that will outlast it?

And, of course, Jabez' influence isn't over yet if you allow his story to inspire you to believe and to pray. His influence will live on if you will open your heart today, especially if you will open that part of your heart that hides shadows of shame and disgrace from the past.

Jabez prayed as if everything depended on God, but he worked as if everything depended on him, and God blessed him beyond his fondest dream. I believe God will bless you the way He blessed Jabez. I do not mean that God will make you rich, but He will richly bless you. In fact, the more of God's rich blessings you have, the less earthly riches appeal to you anyway. When Jabez and Achsah were old, Achsah observed that they had hardly enough possessions to run a household. Jabez, according to his wife, had given away almost every earthly possession, keeping only the Torah, the Holy Scriptures.

God had blessed Jabez financially, but He also blessed his personal life, taking away the disgrace label. He had blessed his family life. God had blessed him intellectually and spiritually through his school. And God gave him a legacy to pass on to the succeeding generations.

God blesses us as He sees fit. He may not make you rich, but He will bless you richly, in the various dimensions of life.

And there you have the lovely and unique story of Jabez. What a story. But in a way, it's not new after all, is it? We might even say that God is in a rut. Isn't He always picking up some nameless nobody who has not the slightest excuse for hope and giving him more than he ever deserved? Isn't Jabez' story your story? Weren't you about as hopeless as Jabez? A poor, lost, hell-deserving sinner, piling disgrace upon disgrace, battered around by forces greater than you could cope with? Isn't that where you were when Jesus found you and lifted you up by His grace and set you on the upward way? And Jabez' history shows us that God's way is the upward way. Jabez' story is my story; it's your story. It is God's story.

I wonder what unexpected, undreamed-of blessing God is going to pour out on you next? Perhaps it is a two-spring ranch or even a new name.

Let us pray in unison the prayer of Jabez as a benediction:

Oh that thou wouldest bless me indeed,
and enlarge my coast,
and that thine hand might be with me,
and that thou wouldest keep me from evil,
that it may not grieve me! (1 Chron. 4:10, KJV).

Learning from Leah

Leah can be a teacher to those whose love loves someone else, and counselor to those who have watched their fondest hopes shrivel and dry up like a raisin in the sun.

SCRIPTURE LESSON: Gen. 29:16-23, 25-28, 30

The worst thing a plain and homely girl can have is not dandruff, or even acne.

The worst thing an ugly girl can have is—a beautiful sister.

Leah was a plain and homely girl. As far as I know, Leah is the only woman whom the Bible carefully designates as hard to look at.

If someone you have just beaten in a chess game says you are ugly, you can discount that.

If your little sister who is mad at you for hogging the TV set calls you ugly, you can disregard that.

But if the Bible, the inspired Word of God, says you are ugly, that pretty well settles it—you are hard to look at.

The Bible is not being unkind when it points out Leah's lack of looks. The Bible writer wants you to know that she made her contributions in spite of a deficit in the typical feminine asset of beauty. Even then, the Bible makes this point indirectly so that the point is made, but not rudely made. Note that the two sisters, Leah and Rachel, are contrasted in verse 17. On the one hand, Rachel was "lovely in form, and beautiful" (NIV). She was gorgeous all over. On the other hand was Leah, described here as "weak-eyed," "tender eyed" (KJV), or of "delicate eye" (see NJKV). In the ancient

Hebrew writings this phrase is sometimes used as a euphemism for an unattractive person, and it is frequently used to describe a person who has a sensitive nature and is constantly weeping. Leah was a young woman who cried a lot. And one thing is certain, she would not likely win any beauty contests while she was bawling her eyes out. Her gorgeous sister was probably the source of many of her tears. Leah had what no plain girl needs—a beautiful sister.

Leah's name didn't help her any either, especially when you remember that normally Old Testament names were intended to describe the dominant character trait of the person. Herbert Lockyer, the man who has analyzed all the names in the Bible, says that the name "Leah" comes from two words. The first means "weary." The second, "wild cow." Put those together and shorten them for everyday use, and you have a young woman called "Tired Cow."

We, like Jacob, have a predilection for beautiful women. Thus, in most of the books and sermons written about Laban, Leah, Rachel, and Jacob, the "tender eyed" Leah is relegated to the role of one of the flat characters who waits in the wings of the center stage on which the gorgeous Rachel prances and performs. But in this sermon we will look at the character and contribution, the losses and the legacy, of the tender-eyed Leah.

Leah could be teacher to all those who have been outshone by a handsome brother or a beautiful sister.

Wedding Bells
(Gen. 29:15-21)

After Jacob had outsmarted his brother Esau and had nabbed the birthright, he made himself scarce. Fleeing from Esau, he made his way to Padanaram, the land of his kinsmen, looking for a wife. There he met Laban and his two daughters, Leah and Rachel. For Jacob, it was love at first sight when he saw the lovely form and beautiful face of the "well favoured" Rachel (v. 17, KJV). He wanted her desperately, but he had no bride price, no dowry to offer. But his credit was good—he worked out an arrangement to pay the bride price on the installment plan. Almost at once he entered into a contract with Laban. He agreed to serve for seven years as a glorified hired hand on the ranch, and he was to receive Rachel as his wife at the end of that time. A seven-year engagement sounds outrageous to us, but to the lovesick Jacob "they seemed . . . but a few days, for the love he had to her" (v. 20, KJV).

At the end of the seven years, the wedding took place. Jacob thought he was marrying Rachel when, after a full day of feasting and drinking, he greeted his veiled bride in the marriage tent (vv. 23-24). But when the first javelins of light from the dawning sun pierced the darkness of the tent, the now sober Jacob discovered that it was not Rachel but Leah with whom he had shared the bridal bed.

The crafty Laban had seized the opportunity to kill two birds with one stone. He had a chance to marry off a plain daughter, and he had found a way to keep Jacob from taking his herds and departing. He wanted the industrious and prosperous Jacob to continue working for him. He figured that he could count on Jacob's passionate love for Rachel to bring this about. He was right. As soon as Jacob confronted him about the wedding fraud, Laban had a plan to suggest (v. 27). The new plan was that if Jacob would agree to work on the ranch for another seven years he could take Rachel as his wife just seven days hence. "It's a deal," Jacob responded.

Thus Leah became a pawn in her father's crafty business deal. She was a voiceless victim. How do you suppose she felt, knowing that her father believed that the only way he could ever marry her off was by trickery? How do you suppose she felt, lying in the bridal tent waiting for Jacob, risking the ultimate humiliation? Do you suppose she was simple enough to think that she could erase Jacob's love for Rachel in this one night of fraudulent love? Could Leah make him see that she was the woman for him?

When the morning came, the answer to all these questions was painfully evident. Leah had risked and had suffered the ultimate humiliation, the ultimate rejection, for at daybreak Jacob was off to strike a bargain for another bride. How the tender-eyed Leah must have wept.

Leah could be teacher to all those whose love loves someone else.

Laban excused his deceptive scheme, telling Jacob that in their land, Padanaram, the oldest daughter must be married before the younger one can be given in marriage. Jacob had fled to Padanaram to escape the anger of Esau. Jacob had flaunted his blatant disregard for the rights of the firstborn when he bilked his brother, Esau, out of the blessing. Now, in this new land, the first bitter lesson he had to learn had to do, strangely enough, with the rights of the firstborn. Leah was the instrument of that lesson.

The only compassionate act with which we can credit Laban was that he made Jacob spend one week with Leah before marrying Rachel. Thus, Leah may have had her husband's attention for a few days. But within a week, Jacob had married Rachel, and Leah's tent became a lonely dwelling.

Leah could be teacher to the lonely.

Seven Children Born in Hope

The Bible says that Leah became the "hated" and "unloved" (NKJV) wife. But, as is His way, God noticed the unloved Leah and gave her children (v. 31). In rapid succession Leah bore her husband four sons. Each birth was a triumph over the beautiful Rachel, who, as yet, had borne no child. In those days and in that part of the world, sons were very precious, and the women who bore them were highly honored. With each new baby, Leah hoped that Jacob would realize her value and make her the honored rather than the unloved wife.

Wait a minute—some of you have fallen off the track. You are saying, "If she was so unloved, where did all these babies come from?" My answer to you is—yes, she had children. Yes, she had sex. Had not Jacob made of her tent a veritable breeding stall? Offspring became a man's status symbol, an important part of an important man's wealth. The fertile Leah was a wealth object, not a loved companion.

Leah could be a teacher to the lost generation of young

people who have not been able to tell the difference between love and sex. Leah could explain all that to them.

Each child of Leah's was born in hope. She gave her sons names that betrayed the aching hunger of her unloved heart. She called her first son Reuben, which means "Behold, a son," and exclaimed, "Surely now my husband will love me" (v. 32). Her second son she named Simeon, which means "hearing," and declared, "The Lord has heard that I am unloved" (v. 33, NKJV). The third son she called Levi, which means "joined" in hope, as she said, "This time will my husband be joined unto me" (v. 34, KJV). Levi was followed by Judah, which means "praise the Lord," surely the exclamation of a woman who still had hope. Leah later bore her fifth son, Issachar, and shortly thereafter gave birth to a sixth son, Zebulun. Her hope for favor was still alive, for Zebulun means "dwelling," and at his birth, Leah exclaimed, "Now will my husband dwell with me" (30:20, KJV).

Leah's handmaiden, Zilpah, bore Jacob two more sons, Gad and Asher. Leah, as Zilpah's mistress, had the privilege of naming her two sons. Leah shows us that in spite of all that she had endured, she had not lost her sense of humor. For when Zilpah's first son came along, Leah named him Gad, saying, "A troop cometh" (30:11, KJV).

Leah bore a daughter too. Her name was Dinah, and she grew up to be a stunningly beautiful young woman. What a sweet reward for the plain Leah. I imagine that every time she had half a chance, she would dress up this little doll and proudly parade her in front of Rachel. You can read Dinah's sad story in Genesis 34. It reminds us that the beautiful have their own set of temptations and problems.

But now, back to Leah. Seven children born in hope. But no number of healthy babies drew Jacob's love to Leah. Rachel had taken her husband and would keep him as long as she lived.

Leah could be teacher to those who have seen a hope deferred to shrivel like a raisin in the sun.

Leah had given all she had to give, but love did not come. This is dramatically demonstrated when Jacob and his family leave Padanaram and head home to face Esau. Afraid that his gift of 580 head of livestock will not appease Esau, Jacob arranges his family and slaves in a precise marching order. Whoever else might miss the significance of the marching order, the tender-eyed Leah could not. Out front rode the two slave girls, the handmaidens, with their children. They were the least valued, the least cherished in Jacob's family. They would bear the brunt of the attack from Esau's archers and spear throwers. They would be the first to be trampled by his horsemen. After the slave girls came Leah, with all those children born in hope. They would be the next to be sacrificed to the swords and arrows of Esau's warriors. At the rear rode beautiful Rachel and her only son, Joseph, under the personal protection of Jacob himself. As Norah Lofts says, "The order of march recorded wordlessly the whole of Leah's sorry history; midway between the bond slaves and the wife, that was her place."

Leah and Jacob Together

It may be that after Rachel died giving birth to Benjamin, Leah finally gained her lifelong desire of being the wife of Jacob's bosom. We do not know whether or not Jacob elevated her after Rachel's death. But of her final triumph we are fully instructed by the Bible. Rachel died and was buried in Bethlehem. Years later, Jacob lay dying in Egypt. He gave his sons strict orders about his burial. He told them to bury him, not with Rachel in Bethlehem, but with Leah at Machpelah. "There," Jacob told his sons, "they buried Abraham and Sarah his wife; there they buried Isaac and Rebekah his wife; and there I buried Leah" (Gen. 49:31, KJV). Leah's sons faithfully carried out their father's wishes. Finally, Leah and Jacob lay side by side. As Edith Deen observes, "Once long ago Leah had bargained for one night of love; now at last the longest night of all was hers." A small triumph indeed.

Leah's Legacy

At first, Leah's life may seem miserable and insignificant

to us. But do not be too quick to trivialize her contributions. Each of her sons founded 1 of the 12 tribes of Israel. Reuben stood in a favored position because he was Jacob's firstborn. Levi became the priestly tribe. His descendants stood as mediators between the people and their God. Their sacred duties brought forgiveness of sin and peace with God. Issachar was known as a productive, agricultural hard worker. Zebulun became the father of sailors, and there is evidence that his clan sailed to America centuries before Columbus was ever born.

Perhaps the son that made Leah most proud was that young lion of a son called Judah. He became the ruler of his brothers, including Rachel's sons. He became the founder of a nation. And from Leah and her son Judah in "the fulness of the time" came Jesus Christ (Gal. 4:4, KJV), who has taken forever the title of "the Lion of the tribe of Judah" (Rev. 5:5)! Yes, Leah must have been proud of that son.

Though Jacob had not chosen Leah, God had chosen Leah to be the ancestress of the King of Kings and Lord of Lords, the Savior of the world!

All the painful struggle of Leah's life takes on enhanced meaning because of Christ. And everything we do, no matter how unimportant it seems, takes on sacramental significance when done in Christ's name and in His service.

Leah lives out a great truth before our eyes. That truth is that God works through all of us, even the disfavored, the unwanted, the unattractive, and the utterly ordinary. Such folks regularly make contributions of lasting importance.

Leah could be teacher to those who think they don't count.

Leah's influence lived on through her sons, and as the years passed, appreciation for her contribution began to grow. When Ruth the Moabitess married Boaz, a descendant of Leah's son Judah, the wedding celebration was climaxed with a chorus by the witnesses that read in part: "The Lord make the woman that is come into thine house like . . . Leah [who] . . . did build the house of Israel" (Ruth 4:11, KJV). And that blessing has become a permanent part of the Jewish wedding ceremony, even up to this very day. Leah made one other contribution to the standard Jewish wedding ceremony too—after the fiasco in Padanaram, only the groom, and no one else, is to lift the veil of the bride.

Leah, Our Teacher

Leah, our teacher for today, instructs us to be faithful, never to give in to the disadvantages that seem to think they own us. Professor Leah also teaches us that what is done to improve the lot of humankind, both in this life and the next, is not reserved for the gifted, the beautiful, the graceful, and the rich and famous alone. But those of us who have weaknesses, those of us who may be unwanted, unloved, or unattractive, can make important contributions for God and good.

Who among us then can be taught by Leah? Only those who

> have felt unattractive
> have had their self-esteem stomped on
> have felt unloved and unwanted
> have been losers in sibling rivalry
> have been victimized by parental favoritism
> have been rejected and humiliated
> have seen fond hopes of the heart shrivel and dry up like a raisin in the sun
> have loved someone who loved someone else better, and those who
> have worked long, hard, and unnoticed behind the scenes without much credit

If, by any chance, there is someone here today who inhabits one or more of these categories, Leah could be teacher to you.

Leah could teach you by her example.

Leah, plain, ordinary Leah, represents the quiet contributors. Those folks who just keep on praying and working and hoping and obeying without any fanfare, glory, medals, or parades. We could use a lot more of those kind of folks in the church, I can tell you.

Leah can teach you by causing you to look for the Leahs in your life.

Who have been the quiet contributors who have brought meaning to your life? I think of a schoolteacher named Jenny Lloyd. She taught in a one-room school up in the badlands of the Dakotas. She only had five students, and they were all brothers and cousins. Finally, the state decided that it could no longer provide a school just for the benefit of one family of wheat farmers out on the plains. They closed the school, and Jenny Lloyd lost her job. But during the short time she taught those five kids, she infected one of the little boys with a love for learning. He cherished what she taught him and wanted to learn more. He went on to Northwest Nazarene College, and then to Nazarene Theological Seminary, and from there to Princeton, where he earned a Ph.D. in Biblical Studies. He still loves to learn and teach, to infect others with a love for learning and a love for the Holy Scriptures. I speak of one of the most gifted and most loved professors at Nazarene Theological Seminary, Dr. Morris Weigelt. His "Leah" was named Jenny Lloyd.

For me, it was an older sister who stayed home from college so that I could go. That was back in the days when there were no such things as government grants and loans for education. At the time, it all seemed so right to me. After all, I was the one with the grade-point average, and I was the one who was "called" to preach. So she stayed home and worked and helped out with the younger kids, and I went off to college, filled with my own self-importance. I'm sure I didn't even say, "Thank you," to her. But you know, she still prays for me every day. I'll not tell you her real name, but you could call her "Leah."

Can you think of any Leahs in your life? They are usually unthanked or underthanked quiet supporters who have helped you make it this far. It is so easy to forget them, to take them for granted. What names and faces has the Holy Spirit brought to your mind in these quiet moments? Do you have some calls to make, some words to speak, some letters to write? When will you take care of this? Set a day this week, a definite day and time.

But that brings us to the last thought from Leah, our teacher.

Leah can urge us today to be a Leah to others.

If the Lord wanted you to be a quiet contributor, a faithful friend, a Leah to someone, who do you suppose it would be? Do you know someone who needs encouragement? Some wavering Christian who needs support? How about someone who needs to hear from you that a past offense is forgiven and forgotten? Do you know someone who has to go a month between compliments? Know anyone who needs a hug? Do you know a lonely person? Someone who is sick or hungry, shut out or shut in? Can you think of someone who needs an unexpected kindness, someone who would really be surprised at a kind deed from you? Is there someone who needs you to expect the best of them? To show them tough love? To whom could you be a "Leah"?

You see, only you can finish this sermon, and you can best finish it by becoming a Leah. I can only leave you with these parting words as you go out to finish this sermon. These words are from the blessing in the Jewish wedding ceremony, slightly edited from the Book of Ruth: "The Lord make [you] like Leah, who did build the house of Israel."

||||||||||||||||||||||||||||||||||||||||

Jephthah: Faithful Keeper of Vows to God

"Beware of vows with 'if' clauses. You can't dicker with God as though He were a cantaloupe vendor at the farmers' market."

SCRIPTURE BACKGROUND: Judg. 10:6—12:7

TEXT: Judg. 11:30-39

In order to study Jephthah, we must whisk ourselves back in time to the dim shadows of antiquity. His deeds, which echo through the corridors of the centuries right on down to us in modern times, were wrought in a primeval era that predates the famous clash of David and Goliath, and long before Solomon wrote and recited poetry to his 1,000 wives and concubines. He lived centuries before Isaiah had his vision of God "high and lifted up" (6:1). Long before Micah thundered that Yahweh loved justice more than His chosen people or the holy hill, Zion, Jephthah committed his deeds of faith and valor. Long before Jonah went on his missionary journey, Jephthah made a few journeys of his own.

But even though Jephthah lived in some twilight time long ago and far away, he has much to teach us about ourselves, religion, and God. More specifically, he teaches us about overcoming obstacles, about robust faith, and about keeping vows. These, particularly the latter, are peculiarly appropriate for us as we stand at the edge of another Lenten season.

Religious vows are much on our minds at this time. Fat Tuesday, when hordes of revelers in places like Rio and New Orleans try to gorge on sinning, is behind us. The 40 days of discipline, vow keeping, and "giving up things for Lent" are upon us. The vows that people make at this time of year range from the righteous to the ridiculous. Just yesterday I heard four college girls talking about what they would sacrifice for Lent. One piously pronounced that she was giving up chocolate for Lent. Then, after a pause that gave her friends time to ponder this weighty vow, she added, "It's bad for my complexion." What great spiritual growth is likely to result from such a self-serving vow! Jephthah, a leader of Israel, will have something to teach us about such vows—but I am getting ahead of myself. Let me tell you about this man, Jephthah.

Jephthah, a Disadvantaged Child

The first disadvantage that Jephthah had to live down was that his mother was a Canaanite prostitute. She lived among Hebrews who disliked Canaanites. Further, she practiced a despised pagan religion, the worship of Chemosh. And, as a prostitute, she had no social standing, no respectability, not even a social security card.

Fortunately, for her and for her son, Jephthah's father was a rich man. His name was Gilead. He was the leader and ruler of the land of Gilead—you remember, Gilead, as in "Is there no balm in Gilead?" (Jer. 8:22). This man cared for Jephthah and his mother. He raised his illegitimate son as one of the family.

But the day came when the old man, Gilead, died. His sons, not wanting to share the inheritance with an illegitimate half brother, kicked Jephthah out of the family. He had to flee for his life. Penniless, he fled to the wilderness of Tob.

What happens to boys who have immoral mothers and who get tossed out on the streets today? More likely than not, they turn to a life of crime, join a gang, and get into trouble of all kinds. This is exactly what happened to young Jephthah. Not much has changed in the last 3,000 years. Young Jephthah became the toughest of the tough. Soon he was the leader of a renegade gang of bandits with a hideout in the wilderness of Tob.

The day came, however, when the Ammonites made war on the land of Gilead. The Gileadites were peace-loving farmers. They had no army, no military training, and hardly any weapons other than a pitchfork or an oxgoad here and there. They were easy prey for the Ammonite warriors. Quickly the Ammonites took 20 Gileadite cities. Things looked as grim as the Berlin wall. The elders of Gilead gathered for a council. What were they to do? Finally they voted unanimously to get on their horses or camels or whatever else they could find and ride swiftly to the land of Tob and beg their half brother, Jephthah, and his band of brigands to come and save them.

Sure enough, they found his hideout and pled with him to come to their rescue. "Come and be our leader," they begged, "that we may fight with the Ammonites" (11:6).

Jephthah responded, "Did you not hate me, and drive me out of my father's house? Why have you come to me now when you are in trouble?" (v. 7).

They offered to make him their general—with five stars.

Jephthah stroked his beard and drawled something like this: "Fellows, I don't think I want to be a general over a bunch of farmers with oxgoads and pitchforks, who have never been in any engagement tougher than the sack race at the Sunday School picnic."

"Oh, but please, we are all going to die . . ."

"Well, like I said," Jephthah replied, "I never cared much for being general, but I have toyed with the idea of being king [they called it judge in those days] of the land of Gilead. So I'll tell you what. If me and my boys come down and fight the Ammonites, and if God delivers them into our hands, I become the new king. Now what do you say to that?"

The half brothers of this bold son of a prostitute must

have looked at each other in thin-lipped disgust. But as they looked toward the plain below, they saw the smoke of 20 burning cities. And, although it must have hurt all over more than any one place, they agreed to Jephthah's proposition.

To make a long story short, Jephthah prayed in faith, believing, and made a solemn vow to God. He led his men out, routed the Ammonites, and took back the 20 cities that had been lost. He rode back in triumph, and he was made president, or judge, of all the land of Gilead.

Jephthah: Better than His Beginnings

Jephthah teaches us that we can be better than our beginnings. Here is a man who started out with great disadvantages, then lost all that he did have. But he turned to God in faith and made a great success of his tattered life. How do you measure up here? Are you better than your beginnings? This subject is worthy of more extensive treatment. But I do not wish to linger here. Jephthah has other things to teach us. Therefore, at this point, I will simply ask you to think for a moment about how you measure up to Jephthah's example of becoming better than your beginnings.

Jephthah: Service Rather than Revenge

Not only does Jephthah teach us that we can be better than our beginnings, but also he becomes a teaching model on how to relate to those who have wronged us. Jephthah's brothers threatened his life, kicked him out of his home, and stole his inheritance. In return, Jephthah saved their lives, their property, and their families. He risked his own life to save theirs. He rendered service rather than revenge to those who had grievously wronged him.

How do you measure up to Jephthah at this point? Would the people who have wronged you testify that you have returned service rather than exacting revenge? That you have risked yourself to save them? Not only do many of us fail to serve those who have wronged us, but also we find it hard to keep from nursing a warm and cozy glowing feeling when they fall. How do you measure up?

Jephthah: His Famous Faith

Not only is Jephthah remembered for overcoming a bad start and returning service for wrong treatment, but also he is famous for his faith. He really believed in the God of Israel. He waged war with a bunch of bandits and a pack of farmhands as his army. But before going out to do battle, he prayed. He trusted God so fully that a miracle resulted. Jephthah is listed in Hebrews 11 as one of the heroes of faith. He prayed and dared to believe that God would answer.

How do you measure up at this point? Some Christians voice routine prayers without ever expecting to receive an answer, let alone a miraculous answer. I heard a preacher say recently to a drowsy congregation, "If God answered your prayers, it would surprise you to death. Some of you would even refuse to believe it and would do everything you could to dig up a 'natural' explanation for it all." How do you measure up on this matter of real faith? Perhaps this point, too, deserves more attention, but let's not dwell here; Jephthah has something more to teach us.

Jephthah: Keeper of Vows

The spiritual history of most persons could be described as a string of broken vows. The landscape of their lives is strewn with the wreckage of broken vows to God and man. But this was not the case with Jephthah. He took his religious vows very seriously. And it is for his keeping of vows that he is most famous. When he prayed for God to deliver the Ammonites into his hand, he made a solemn vow to God, and he kept it. Even though it cost him deep anguish, he kept it. Jephthah's vow is recorded in verses 30-31 of the 11th chapter of Judges: "If thou wilt give the Ammonites into my hand, then whoever comes forth from the doors of my house to meet me, when I return victorious from the

Ammonites, shall be the Lord's, *and I will offer him up for a burnt offering*" (italics added).

Victory! The sweet-tasting wine of winning! Jephthah leads his army back. Glad whoops of triumph punctuate the march. Jephthah, riding at the front of this happy parade, is not thinking of his vow, he is having a great celebration. Word of his victory has preceded him. The women and children of the city have already organized a victory reception. Jephthah can hear the music even before he can see the dancing girls with their tambourines. But as they near the glad reception, Jephthah remembers his vow. He remembers, because the first tambourine dancer, the lovely young maiden leading the dance troupe, is Sheilah—Sheilah, his only child. Jephthah's heart breaks. He cries out, "Alas, my daughter! you have brought me very low . . . for I have opened my mouth to the Lord, and I cannot take back my vow" (Judg. 11:35). Ancient Jewish accounts of this tragic event record that he also said, "Rightly was the name Sheilah, the one who is demanded, given to thee, that thou shouldst be offered up as a sacrifice."

The historical records say that Sheilah pled with her father, but in the end he stuck to his vow, saying, "I . . . uttered a vow, I cannot take it back." He gave her 60 days to mourn, but as verse 39 tells us, "At the end of two months, she returned to her father, who did with her according to his vow."

Some people today, who cannot cope with the awful brutality of those primitive times, have tried hard to take the death out of this story. A good man of faith like Jephthah would not have killed his daughter; he probably just sent her to the nearest thing there was to a nunnery in those days. But the rabbinical writings, the historical writers closest to this event in time, have no doubt whatever that, true to his vow, Jephthah offered his daughter, Sheilah, as a burnt offering. What a horrible scene. Yet Jephthah kept his vow. He was no bleeding heart sentimentalist who would back down on a vow to God.

How do you measure up to Jephthah on this matter of vow keeping? What is your record? Do you promise God one thing and do another? Perhaps you do not take your vows to God as seriously as Jephthah. Would you have had the wherewithal to keep that vow that Jephthah kept? *Just how do you measure up to Jephthah here?*

Not very well, I hope!

I certainly hope you have more sense than to keep a vow like that. Jephthah was stupid to keep it—don't you agree?

Wait just a minute, I hear some of you saying. Jephthah is one of the heroes in the "faith chapter." He teaches us a lot of good things!

What you say is true. We admire Jephthah when he overcomes his bad start in life.

We admire him for risking his own life to save the people who had so grievously wronged him.

We certainly admire his faith, a faith so strong that he believed God would deliver a well-equipped army into the hands of his vagabond warriors.

But we must deplore his foolish, stupid, misguided vow. And we deplore even more his stubborn keeping of it.

This is not so hard to take when we remember that other heroes of faith were not always models worth imitating. Abraham is a model for us when he answered God's call to leave his pleasant surroundings and go to a strange land. But he is not a model for us when, confronted by some fellows who he thought would kill him so that they could nab his wife, he lied and called his wife his sister. In order to save his skin, he put his wife to risk, and she was kidnapped and dragged off to the king's harem. Then there is Samson— a model for us when he lived for God but not when he pursued his lecherous cravings. Consider David. He is a model for us when, under the inspiration of the Spirit, he pens the 23rd psalm; but his lust for Bathsheba is not worthy of imitation.

It is the same with Jephthah. At his best he is our model, but at his worst he is a horrible example. At first reading, most people, including most preachers who speak about him, think they must find some way to justify his vow and its terrible outcome. That is wrong; when it comes to this stupid and selfish vow, Jephthah is no more a good example for us than lying Abraham, carousing Samson, or lustful David.

Jephthah's Vow Examined

1. Jephthah's vow was improper because *it required someone else to sacrifice more than its maker*. Jephthah had to give up something dear to him, but poor Sheilah had to give up her life so that her father could feel religious.

Sheilah tried everything to get her father to change his mind. In Judges 11 she seems quite submissive to the vow. "Do to me according to what has gone forth from your mouth" (v. 36), she says. But the rabbinical writings, which tell a longer version of the story, point out that she said this believing that God would do for her what He had done for Isaac when Abraham was about to offer him on Mount Moriah. God would provide himself another "lamb," she thought. She also was patient, fully believing that her father would come to realize that God in His rescue of Isaac had forever forbidden His people to make human sacrifices. But it seems that not even God can stop the religiously stubborn person.

Sheilah's next move was to try to reason with her father. "When my father vowed his heedless vow, he did not have me in mind," she pled. She was right, of course. Jephthah had himself in mind, not his daughter. Further, she reasoned with him from Scripture. She pointed out to him that when Jacob promised to give 10 percent of all that he had, he did not sacrifice 1 of his 12 sons. In addition, she pointed out to him that the Torah spoke only of animal sacrifices. But it takes more than reason to convince a misguided and stubborn person who has blamed his stupidity on God.

Jephthah did permit Sheilah to visit the sages for counsel about the legality of the vow. But these cowardly men were so afraid to offend a bloodthirsty bandit king that they spoke in riddles, saying nothing. The rabbinical writers declare that the high priest, Phineas, could have settled the matter in a moment, but he was too proud to approach a half-breed judge. On the other hand, Jephthah could have consulted the high priest on his own, but he decided that in his newfound royalty he was too good to seek advice from a commoner like Phineas. So the rivalry between Jephthah and Phineas caused the death of a young lady.

Sheilah prayed about her fate. God spoke to her, the ancient writers say, telling her, "I know her [Sheilah] to be wiser than her father, and all the wise men, and now her soul shall be accepted at her request, and her death shall be very precious before My face all the time." It seems that not even God can change the mind of a stubborn fool glued to a stupid vow.

2. Jephthah's vow was improper because *by the laws of God and man it was illegal.*

Ever since Abraham had been forbidden to slay his son on Mount Moriah, the Israelites had known that human sacrifice was taboo. In other ancient societies right on up into the Christian era, fathers had the right to kill their children if they wanted to—but that was never the case with God's chosen people.

This being the case, where would Jephthah go to have his daughter sacrificed? Certainly no true priest of Jehovah would have sacrificed her. He had to backslide to do it. And that is exactly what he did, according to the ancient writers who record this sorrowful tale. He reverted to the religion of his Canaanite mother who worshiped Chemosh—and human sacrifice was really big with Chemosh. In the cavernous temple built to him was a huge idol, his terrible image. Each outstretched palm of the idol formed a huge furnace. At the harvest festival each year, a roaring fire was kindled in each palm. Then, if Chemosh demanded it through his priests, any man and wife who that year had brought forth a first-born child had to march forward at the height of the frenzied ceremonies and throw their baby into one of those flaming palm-furnaces. They had to burn their baby in order to prove they loved their god more than any earthly thing. They would then be honored as being truly religious.

What a horrid practice. This is probably where Jephthah got the crazy idea of sacrificing his daughter anyway.

He was a serious man, but the popular pagan religion of the times had, in his mind, been hopelessly mixed with the religion of the true God. He didn't know where one ended and the other began. This led him to carry out an unlawful vow. Even if the vow had been legal, he could have redeemed his daughter with a payment of 30 pieces of silver. But who can stop a stubborn fool glued to a stupid vow? Besides, 30 pieces of silver is a lot of money; silver doesn't grow on trees, you know.

3. Jephthah's vow was improper because *it was a vow that God would not recognize.*

The historical writers assert that God was angered by the vow. They report that God raised the question, "What if a dog is the first one to meet him after his victory? Will he offer Me a dog?" It is interesting to note that the Bible does not say that God was pleased with the bargain Jephthah tried to strike. Perhaps the rabbis are right. They report that God said through His messenger, "I will surely deliver My people, not for Jephthah's sake, but for the sake of the prayers of Israel." The prayers of Israel are summarized in Judg. 10:15, "And the people of Israel said to the Lord, 'We have sinned; do to us whatever seems good to thee; only deliver us, we pray thee, this day.' "

Therefore, it is possible, even likely, that God did not recognize Jephthah's vow at all. But be that as it may, we know that many people make vows that God himself does not recognize. Jesus named one. In New Testament times, one could get out of his responsibility to provide for his aging parents by making out a Corban vow, or will. Under this arrangement, a man "willed" all his earthly possessions to the Temple. He could live off them as long as he lived, but no one else could touch them. If his aging parents were starving and needed some of his money, he could say, "Sorry, folks, I'd love to help you, but you know that I have promised all my money to God's Temple." Jesus declared that God neither wanted nor recognized such promises.

I spoke the other day with a district superintendent about a certain pastor. His career as a pastor has been a failure. He has practically wrecked three churches. He ought to go into another line of work. I think he has proven that he does not have the gifts and graces required for pastoral ministry. When asked about his call to ministry, however, he declares that he cannot give up preaching. He admits he doesn't enjoy the work. But he believes he is bound to do it. His call to ministry came in a firefight in Vietnam. Under intense fire from the enemy, he promised God that he would be a preacher if only he could survive the battle. He survived —which may be more than one can say for the churches he has tried to serve. Was not his a vow that God did not recognize, let alone require?

4. Jephthah's vow was improper because *it was a self-serving vow with an "if" clause.*

Most "if clause" vows turn out to be self-serving. Jephthah's certainly was. Many "if clause" vows trivialize God. It may come as a surprise to you, but you cannot bargain, dicker, and haggle with God as though He were a cantaloupe vendor at the farmers' market. Most "if clause" vows turn out to be sub-Christian.

Look closer at the social and psychological factors at work in Jephthah's stubborn decision to sacrifice his daughter. Sheilah's pleading for her life must have broken Jephthah's heart. Surely all the father in him made him want to take her in his arms and say, "I don't care what I said before. My only child, I believe you are a gift from God. I can't go through with it! I won't! They can call me anything they like. They can throw me out as judge, but, my precious Sheilah, I will never take your life."

But he did not say that. Why? Because he was devout? Not likely. He wanted his daughter, but he wanted to be king (or judge, or president, or head honcho) more. He would rather give up his daughter than give up being king.

The bottom line here for Jephthah was that if he broke his public vow to God and anything bad happened, they wouldn't let him be king anymore. And how this outcast's ego wanted to be king—all that power and respect and glory—he could not give it up.

You see, the popular folk theology of the day held that everything that happened was a reaction of some god to the way people were behaving. Remember when the pagan sailors found out that Jonah was running away from God—they threw him right out into the ocean. Jephthah faced a similar fate. If an epidemic occurred, if a tornado, or earthquake, or an invasion occurred, the public would surely say it was because their "leader" had not kept his vow to Jehovah. Then they would kill both Jephthah and Sheilah. But, he reasoned, better her than both of us.

Remember that Jephthah had overcome a lot to be king. He could not easily give it up. How the shame of his illegitimate birth and mixed ancestry had burned like molten lead in his veins. How bitter poverty had eaten like a cancer at his self-respect. How his expulsion from his father's house had hurt. He had been thrown out before—he just could not stand it again. How he wanted to be king.

So, in the end, he chose to lose his daughter rather than his public image. I don't suppose that he was the last parent to make such a choice.

So What Does This Mean to Me?

Jephthah teaches us to

• be done with religious vows that require others to sacrifice more than we.

• avoid vows that break the spirit of the laws of God.

• renounce the vows that God neither requires nor recognizes.

• walk away from all self-serving vows with "if" clauses.

• stop trying to bargain with God as though He were a cantaloupe vendor.

I think I am preaching today to a lot of people who have a long backlog of immature vows that have been broken. I think the guilt of all this has you spiritually handcuffed. Your failures are ever before you, dampening your spirit, crushing your hopes. What am I to do? you ask. I'll tell you what to do about those stupid, immature, self-serving bargains, those improper vows of your past! Walk away from them! Forget them! They have tyrannized your life too long already! Celebrate a new freedom from them. Ask God to deliver you from the false bondage to which you have submitted. Be free! Celebrate!

"That's wonderful! That sets me free!" I hear you say. "I've got at least a dozen vows I'm walking away from. They were probably all immature, stupid, self-serving vows—just like you said. Now I'm free to do whatever I want."

No, no. Wait a minute. I think you misunderstood me.

You see, the flaw that inhabits the vows we have been talking about is not that they required too much of you. Quite the opposite. The problem is that they require too little of you. They are too easy. They represent a sort of piecemeal approach to Christianity. You get in a jam and promise that if He gets you out, you will visit the senior citizens home on Christmas. Lord, get me a victory, and I'll give $1,000 to missions. Help me win the lottery, and I will triple tithe—after taxes, of course. It's a life of little bargains with God.

Really, the Christian life is more simple than that. It's not a complex series of appropriate vows and bargains. What God wants is not your pledges, promises, and vows to do good deeds. No, He wants a lot more than that. And He wants it all in one transaction. He wants you—not installment plan good deeds. He wants you, all of you.

The saints in the Middle Ages called it self-donation. They meant simply donating your whole self to God. What does the Lord need with little vows? What He wants is the total you. He wants you to donate your whole being, all that you are, and all that you do. The *Manual of the Church of the Nazarene* calls this "complete devotement." Some Christians call it self-surrender. Whatever you call it, we know that Christianity will not work any other way. The genius of Christianity is in the transcendence of self and selfishness by being crucified with Christ and resurrected with Him in order that you, like Christ, can live for God by living not for yourself but for others. The believer who has donated himself to God can affirm the proclamation of Paul in Col. 3:3, "For you have died, and your life is hid with Christ in God." He can also sense, even if explanation is elusive, the meaningful mystery in these words from Colossians, "You were also raised with him through faith" (2:12).

So let us be done with piecemeal vows to give up chocolate for Lent and other self-serving trivialities. Instead, let us donate to Him all that we have and are. Perhaps there is no better way to move toward this goal than to adopt as our own John Wesley's prayer of consecration. Would you claim this prayer, pray it daily during the coming weeks?

O Lord Jesus, I give thee my body,
my soul, my substance, my fame, my friends,
my liberty, and my life.
Dispose of me and of all that is mine,
as it seems best unto thee.
I am not now mine, but thine: therefore
claim me as thy right, keep me as thy charge,
and love me as thy child.
Fight for me when I am assaulted, heal me
when I am wounded, and revive me when I am destroyed.

||||||||||||||||||||||||||||||||||||||||||||

Abner: The Great and Foolish Warrior

"Sin is real and the stakes are high."

SCRIPTURE LESSON: 2 Sam. 3:26-38

And they buried Abner in Hebron: and the king lifted up his voice, and wept at the grave of Abner; and all the people wept. And the king lamented over Abner, and said,
Died Abner as a fool dieth?
Thy hands were not bound,
nor thy feet put into fetters:
as a man falleth before wicked men, so fellest thou.
(2 Sam. 3:32-34, KJV)

Abner was a mighty warrior. He lived in the days of King Saul, Israel's first king, and in the days of the young King David. When Saul died, falling on his own sword rather than submitting to capture and torture by the Philistines, the nation was dragged into civil war over who should succeed Saul as king. One faction said, "David is the man." Another faction crowned Ishbosheth (Saul's son) king. Thus the nation was divided. Ishbosheth ruled one part and David, with headquarters in Hebron, ruled the other part.

Naturally, they decided that they would have to stage a war to settle the issue of who would be the real king. David had a fine corps of troops headed by Joab, his general. Ishbosheth had a fine general, too, perhaps the finest warrior in all the land, Abner.

By the pool of Gibeah, the two armies met. It was decided that they would talk first and fight later. The talks gave birth to a limited battle plan—one that would not risk so many men, especially officers. The two generals talked for a while, then someone said something like this: "How about you picking your 12 best fighters, and I'll pick my 12 best. If your guys can whip my guys, then your candidate can be king; if my guys whip yours, then my candidate gets to be king." It sounded like a good plan to the generals; after all, it was a hot day. If you really had to go to battle, you could get all hot and sweaty out there. Besides, somebody could get hurt.

At the prearranged signal, Abner's dozen clashed with Joab's dozen on the "Field of Blades," as it came to be known, with the two armies standing like fans at a football game on both sides of the field. But the game ended in a tie. The Bible says that each of the 24 brave warriors seized his opponent by the beard and stabbed him with his sword. All 24 fell down dead. Having no rules on how to break a tie (no overtime period or anything like that), the two armies charged into a full-scale battle. Joab, David's general, lost 20 men, but they killed 360 of Abner's finest.

Enter Asahel. Asahel was a mere boy, a teenager, barely old enough to serve in the army. He was, however, a highly motivated soldier. He had something to prove. After all, he had two big brothers in this army. His brother, Abishai, was an officer—at least a full colonel. His other brother was Joab, the general of David's army. When you are a buck private, and your two brothers are the top ranking officers, you have something to prove. And so it was with young Asahel.

In the battle at the Field of Blades Asahel saw his opportunity to do some heavyweight impressing. Doubtless he had rehearsed the scene in his mind many times. When Abner's army was routed, Asahel's plan took form. He would chase down the opposing general, Abner, kill him, cut off his head, and come swaggering back into camp and fling the general's head at the feet of his big brothers. What an impression that would make! He would get some bars to wear on his shoulders, and from then on he would be a mighty warrior—maybe even more glorious than his brothers.

He set his sights on the retreating Abner. The Bible says that Asahel could run like a deer. Quickly he gained ground on Abner. Standing on a knoll, Abner looked back at his pursuer. He thought he recognized him. "Is that you, Asahel?"

"It's me, all right. And I am going to take your head. You know you cannot outrun me. You're a dead man, Abner."

"Listen, kid," Abner called back (not a prudent way to address a teenager with a spear in his hand), "go chase someone else—go after a corporal, or a second lieutenant or something. But don't follow me. Don't make me kill you, kid. If I have to kill a boy warrior like you, I could never look your brothers in the face."

"You are my ticket to glory, Abner. You cannot escape."

Asahel pushed the pursuit. Several times Abner stopped and warned Asahel to turn aside. But he would not. Soon the fleet-footed youth caught up with his prey. The two men looked each other in the eye on that dusty trail. Once more, Abner asked Asahel to give it up. But Asahel thought these were the words of a scared man. He made his move, and Abner, great and powerful warrior that he was, struck Asahel down with one blow. The Bible says that he did not even use the sharp end of his spear but struck him with the "hinderend" part of the weapon (the handle), and smote him so hard that the spear handle smashed through his fifth rib and came out his back. Asahel's dream of glory died as his lifeblood was soaked up by the dust and sand on that desert trail.

Asahel's body was carried back to the tent of his brothers. There, Joab and Abishai took a blood oath to avenge their brother's blood, which cried out to them from the ground. From then on, one thing dominated their minds. Only one thing could cleanse the red stain from their family's honor. They had to kill Abner. This they must do even if other very important things had to be put off.

Meanwhile, back at the ranch, Abner arrives back home. He is exhausted, humiliated, defeated. His army is whipped and scattered, his nation teetering on the brink of disaster, and his ego shattered like a thrown egg. So what does a man do at a time like this? Read the *Wall Street Journal?* Watch "Monday Night Football"? Go bowling? No. Every man here today knows what to do at such a time, and that's what Abner did. He sought out some female companionship. He went to see his girlfriend, Rizpah.

Rizpah must have been quite a woman. When Saul had been king, he paid her rent. Now the would-be king, Ishbosheth, paid her rent, but General Abner had an eye for her too.

Unfortunately, King Ishbosheth found out that Abner and Rizpah had spent the evening together. I don't know how he found out. Perhaps Ishbosheth was in need of female companionship, too, and drove by only to find Abner's chariot parked in the drive.

This was more than just two men fighting for the charms of the same woman—much more. To understand the significance of the Abner-Rizpah date, one must remember the politics of those times. In those days, if you wanted to be king in the place of the man then on the throne, you did not go down to the county courthouse and file as a candidate in the next election. The quickest way to serve public notice that you were taking the king's job was to take the king's women.

Remember when Absalom ousted David, his father, from the throne. You've read the story in the Bible. One of the first things in the public campaign was to move David's harem to temporary quarters in the public street so that all the citizens could see that it was Absalom, not David, who was visiting the royal harem.

Later, when Solomon was king, his brother Adonijah asked for permission to marry Abishag—a fatal mistake. You see, when David was old and feeble and dying, his advisers thought that the old king might be helpfully comforted if they could find a sweet young thing to warm his bed. Abishag was the beautiful young woman selected, and for a short time she served as David's nurse and bed warmer. Years later, Adonijah wanted to marry this woman and asked his brother, King Solomon, for permission to do so. To Solomon, this was a direct political challenge. He sent his secret police with orders to kill his brother. Adonijah fled and took refuge in a house of worship, thinking they would not murder him in the very presence of the Deity. He was wrong. They chopped him down right there in the sanctuary.

So you see, Abner's liaison with Rizpah was a bold political challenge to Ishbosheth. This act was a clear announcement that Abner was tired of being general and wanted to be king. At once, Ishbosheth had Abner dragged before him, and he bawled him out good. But things took a strange turn. Abner would not be disciplined. "How dare you treat me like a dead dog's head over this woman?" he challenged. "Why, if it were not for me and my troops, not only would you have no throne, but you would not even have a head. The only thing standing between you and David's butchers is me and my men. If you don't get off my case, and I mean now, I will just step aside and let David have the country. How long do you think you would last?"

Ishbosheth backed down, and Abner left in a huff. And the more he thought about his threat, the more he liked the idea. By now he knew that he did not have the manpower to resist David's army. He had a weak king on the throne who could not even protect his own concubines. Maybe the prudent thing to do would be to make an arrangement to deliver Ishbosheth's part of the kingdom into David's hands. He might even save his own life in the process. The life expectancy of defeated generals in those days was probably something like two or three minutes.

Abner then makes a secret visit to David's capital, Hebron. He makes all the arrangements with David. Plans are made in detail for Abner to deliver Ishbosheth into David's hands. It's a done deal. Abner leaves and starts his long journey home.

He has hardly gotten out of sight of the city when Joab and Abishai come in from "pursuing a troop." "Guess who just left town," someone said to them. "The man who brutally murdered your kid brother, that's who. He's been here all day working out plans to set David up as king of all Israel, or so they say."

Joab, however, believed that Abner had no such intention and was in Hebron merely to spy out David's stronghold, or so he said. Quickly he forged a message on the royal stationery and sent a fast messenger to catch up with Abner. Abner was told that the message was from David. Some new developments had occurred, and more plans had to be made at once. So Abner returned to Hebron. At the edge of the city, just outside the main gate, he saw David's military leaders, Joab and Abishai. They beckoned to him. Thinking that they wanted to confer further about the plan to deliver the land to David, he walked right up to them. They seized him and stabbed him in the fifth rib, the same spot where he had delivered the fatal blow to Asahel, their brother. Abner fell dead.

David arranged a state funeral for Abner. He publicly wept over Abner's casket. Some said that David was in real grief; others said it was a political act (he didn't want the followers of Ishbosheth and Abner to think he had treacherously killed their hero). The crowd gathered for the funeral. The main part of the ceremony was a funeral dirge, a funeral song written by David, the poet-king. The words to the song are preserved for us in 2 Sam. 3:33-34. Paraphrased, they go like this

> *Oh, Abner, did you not die the death of a fool?*
> *Your hands were not bound,*
> *Your feet were not tied.*
> *As an unarmed man falls before wicked outlaws,*
> *So you fell.*

After this song had been sung, David gave a eulogy. It is summarized for us in verse 38: "Know ye not that there is a prince and a great man fallen this day in Israel?" (KJV).

Reflections on the Tragic and Foolish Death of Abner

When we analyze Abner's story, we must admit that David was right. Abner died a needless, tragic, foolish death. The *Revised Standard Version* translates the first line of David's song, "Should Abner die as a fool dies?" The answer is, No, he should not—but he did. Let's look at the facts in this case.

Abner died as a fool dies because he listened to a false messenger.

Joab sent a message to Abner, asking him to return to the city to talk further with David. The message seemed reasonable, it sounded official, and appeared to be a good idea—but it was false. And it cost Abner his life.

There are plenty of false messengers today. Abner was not the last person to listen to a false messenger. Some of you here today have done your share of listening to false messengers. Some of you may at this moment be under the spell of a false messenger of some kind. The false messengers that have been bending your ear may be as brazen as the "Playboy philosophy" or as pious as the "theology of prosperity." In either case, the result will be as tragic as the foolish death of Abner if you keep on listening.

Some false messengers afoot in the land include:

1. The "Playboy philosophy," which, according to Hugh Hefner, is that "life is an end in itself, and pleasure is preferable to pain." Therefore, if it feels good, do it. This was the philosophy that fueled the sexual revolution of the '60s and '70s. And it has left us the heritage, rather the foul residue, of epidemic waves of herpes and AIDS—just to cite two by-products of this false messenger. And who can count the broken hearts, shattered families, fatherless children, drug addictions, and the like with which this frantic search for freedom from all moral restraint endowed us.

Janis Joplin, who died from multiple overdoses of heroin, alcohol, and Valium before her best-known record came out, spoke for that generation, which believed a false messenger touting sexual freedom. Janis, a sad and pathetic figure, voiced their collective discovery: "Freedom's just another word for nothing left to lose."

The Playboy philosophy was then and is now wrapped in a package as pretty as a valentine. But someone put a snake in the valentine box. It appears sweet, cute, desirable, satisfying, but in the end it is deadly. E. Stanley Jones once said, "The Christian way is built into man. You may go against it, but sooner or later you end up with hell on your hands."

2. Legalism, on the other hand, is a false messenger too. There are those who really believe that if they keep some man-made code, they can earn their salvation. These pious Pharisees are also listening to the seductive whispers of a false messenger. Frequently, everything about them is right—except their attitude. They aptly fit the description that Mark Twain made of one of his acquaintances: "He was a good man in the worst sense of the term." I have met some of these folk who seem to be plagued with one over-whelming dread, a tense fear that someone, somewhere, is having a good time. But legalism is a false messenger. Strait-laced strutting, meticulous code keeping, picking thorns and tossing away roses, and going through life with a face that looks like a hatchet dipped in vinegar doesn't save anybody. People are saved by the grace of God in Christ, not by works.

3. Sanctified selfishness is another false messenger. The very heart of sin is selfishness. It can get glossed over quite quickly by the merchants of "warm fuzzies" and "sloppy agape" who coach us that the only thing in life is to seek our own self-fulfillment, achieve our own self-actualization, and enhance our own self-esteem. All of these can be good, but they fit so nicely in the shrine of our inner heart, which we reserve for the idols before which we bow down in secret. Look at the life of Jesus. Would you say that His was a life of self-fulfillment, self-actualization? He is our Pattern, you know. True Christianity cannot be separated from self-denial, self-surrender, or, as the medieval saints used to call it, self-donation. Read Matthew 16:24; Mark 8:34; Luke 9:23 before you go to your next class on "winning through intimidation."

4. The "theology of prosperity" is another false messenger. I have known this all along. I knew it even when a woman televangelist looked at me with those big, mascara-clotted eyes and gave me a caked-cosmetic cracking smile and told me, "It's God's will for you to be rich!" It did not

take the fall of a dozen televangelists for me to know this was wrong, for some of Christ's most noble servants on earth have lived and died in poverty. Were they out of God's will? Even when I heard a minister in my own denomination preach a sermon called "Give to Get," I had my doubts. I was really troubled when he told the congregation that you didn't even have to be a Christian to make it work. The hearers were told that if they gave to that church, God would make them prosperous even if they rejected the crucified Christ. It would be easier if all the false messengers were outside the church.

5. I will mention only one more false messenger today: worldliness. You hear a lot of preaching against worldliness, but not often do you hear it properly defined. I'll try. Worldliness is making something less than God your ultimate *good*. To be worldly is to invest some created thing with God value. When a person makes money, power, or success the hub of his life, it is a clear case of idolatry, that is to say, worldliness. It is not so clear but nevertheless a true case of worldliness when a person makes a marriage partner or a Christian institution, like a church or a school, his ultimate good. Even good things promoted to God value are false messengers of worldliness. Are you a worldly person? I do not know. But it may be profitable to reflect on the question, "What is the one thing I cannot live without?" The worldly person's end, like Abner's, is tragically foolish. One can so pursue worldly idols that he ends up saying, like Satan in *Paradise Lost*, "Evil, be thou my good."

But back to Abner. He listened to a false messenger, and it cost him his life. By analogy, his example reminds us that it is possible for us to lose our life and our soul by listening to false messengers. But how can I avoid them? False messengers seem to be everywhere. I know. It's a bit like a banker trying to avoid counterfeit bills. Some of them look so real. I read a 24-page booklet that the Federal Reserve Bank put out to help bank employees determine whether a piece of currency was genuine or not. One test after another was recommended for 23 pages. Then, after all that, the government warned that, even after all these checks had been made, you still might not be able to tell whether or not the bill being examined was genuine or counterfeit. The only way you can tell for sure, the booklet said, is to compare it with one that you know is good.

You know, when any philosophy of life is recommended to me, be it new and revolutionary or old and unexamined, I do what the Federal Reserve recommended. I compare it with one I know is good—the biblical one.

Abner died as a fool dies because he listened to a false messenger.

Consider this too: *Abner died as a fool dies because he trusted his sworn enemy.*

Though Abner knew that Joab and Abishai had taken a blood oath to kill him, he walked right up to them the way you would approach an old friend. He died because he trusted his sworn enemy.

How often people today put their trust in things that destroy them. Allen Ginsberg bet on the cultural revolution of his era, the '50s and the '60s. He was probably the greatest of the "beat generation" poets. In the end, however, he declared, "Life's a long headache in a noisy street." Then there is Frank Sinatra, a man with all the things people dream of—money, fame, popularity—you name it, Sinatra has it. Yet his philosophy of life, revealed in an interview, is, "I'm for anything that will get you through the night, be it prayer, pills, or a bottle of Jack Daniels." How frequently the rich and famous live out the classic element expressed in Edwin Arlington Robinson's *Richard Cory.*

> *Whenever Richard Cory went down town*
> *We people on the pavement looked at him:*
> *He was a gentleman from sole to crown,*
> *Clean favored and imperially slim.*
>
> *And he was always quietly arrayed,*
> *And he was always human when he talked:*
> *But still he fluttered pulses when he said,*
> *"Good morning," and he glittered when he walked.*

And he was rich—yes, richer than a king—
And admirably schooled in every grace:
In fine, we thought that he was everything
To make us wish that we were in his place.

So on we worked, and waited for the light.
And went without the meat, and cursed the bread:
And Richard Cory, one calm summer night,
Went home and put a bullet through his head.

From *The Children of the Night,* by Edwin Arlington Robinson (New York: Charles Scribner's Sons, 1897).

But ordinary people trust the wrong things too. A young woman, a Hollywood starlet, who wanted the fame and glory the rich so often trust, but could not get it, left a suicide note that read, "I wanted caviar, but all I could get was boiled cabbage." I remember sadly a Ph.D., a professor in a midwestern university. My wife was one of his students. He knew she was a minister's wife. Sometimes they spoke of religion. One day he told her with the remorse of a man who knows it's too late, "I turned my back on the Bible and on my parents' religion. And now I am a zero, a cipher, a nothing."

People, rich and poor, make Abner's mistake. The tragic mistake of trusting their sworn enemy. So often it comes in the form of some promising sinful pursuit. The list of examples of people who leaned their ladder on the wrong wall, who trusted the pursuit of pleasure or position to bring satisfaction but found emptiness, could go on and on. Like Abner, they trusted what turned out to be their sworn enemy.

Compare the examples cited earlier, however, with those who trust in Christ. My friend Earl Wolf had a sister who lived in the state of Pennsylvania. She fought a long battle with cancer, finally dying a painful death. Earl made the trip from Missouri to attend her funeral. While he was there, he spent some time leafing through his sister's Bible. He found this handwritten poem tucked in it.

83

Often on the Rock I tremble,
Faint of heart and weak of knee,
But the steadfast Rock of Ages
Never trembles under me.

What a difference Christ makes, even in the most adverse circumstances. Trust Christ—not your sworn enemies: Satan, sin, and selfishness.

As David said, *Abner died as a fool dies because his hands were not bound, and his feet were not put into fetters.*

Abner had two strong hands, the hands of a mighty warrior, but he did not defend himself. He had two strong legs, two strong feet, but he did not flee those bloodthirsty brothers. He also had a band of 20 men with him. But he left the safety of their numbers and strolled up to his sworn enemies.

In other words, Abner had at his disposal the wherewithal to save his life. You too, by God's grace, providence, and gifts, have at your disposal the wherewithal to save your soul. You have the wherewithal to choose God and good. You do not have to be a slave to sin. Jesus Christ saves sinners—and He beckons you.

The Bible treats human beings as free and responsible. That goes against the popular teachings of behaviorism and determinism on which much of the modern philosophy of life is built. Determinists tell us that environment shapes the person. We are not free, they say, but we are just what society and environment makes us. Freedom is a myth, they declare, and therefore responsibility is a myth too.

B. F. Skinner, one of the leaders of this school of thought, declares that praise and blame are out of order. If a man becomes a self-sacrificing missionary, he is not to be praised or honored. If another man becomes a wicked murderer, he is not to be blamed. Both men turned out to be exactly what environment made of them—nothing more, nothing less. Sadly enough, a great deal of the social science and educational theory today assumes that Skinner is right.

Recently I watched a Kansas City television reporter interview a social worker. Some outrageous cases of child abuse had been in the news. The reporter asked the social worker why some parents abuse their children. She answered by saying six times in a 90-second film clip, "They really have no choice." Doubtless they had been abused as children and, being shaped entirely by their environment, "They really had no choice," she explained.

The problem is that this unbiblical foolishness is accepted by the general public. Millions of Americans really believe that they cannot help themselves. When they have trouble, they think it is society's fault, not theirs. "Dad didn't take me fishing often enough," "Mom did not read me stories when I was little," "My brothers and sisters hated me"—these are the types of things these people say all the time. They come up with excuses for all kinds of failures, sins, irresponsibilities, and crimes.

But this is not the biblical doctrine of humankind. In the Word of God, you are treated as a free person and held accountable for your conduct. God has placed at your disposal the wherewithal to save your soul. If you lose your soul and spend eternity in hell, it will not be your pastor's fault. It will not be your husband's fault. It will not be your wife's fault—nor anybody else's fault. It will be your fault. Whatever your situation, God provides you with the grace and opportunity whereby your soul can be saved. Abner died as a fool dies because, although he had the means at his fingertips to save his life, he just stood there. He did not act!

A fourth and last insight into Abner's story also confirms David's analysis: *Abner died as a fool dies because of where he died.*

Abner died just outside the gate of the city of Hebron. I have meditated at his grave in that city. In Abner's time, Hebron was a very special city. There were only five others like it in the world. You see, Hebron was a city of refuge—and Abner died just a step or two outside its main gate. A city of refuge was a safe place. If you had killed someone by accident or in self-defense, you could go to the city of refuge, and they had to grant you asylum. No one could take vengeance on you there. In the city of refuge, you were guaranteed a fair trial.

Poor Abner—so near and yet so far. He died as a fool dies because he could have stepped inside the city and saved his life. But he dallied in the gate and yielded his life to his sworn enemies.

By analogy, Abner teaches us a chilling truth. It is possible to be ever so close to giving your life to Christ but to putter around until it is too late. You can attend church, read the Bible some, spend a lot of time around religious people, admire Christ, and be "almost persuaded" but still lose your soul, still end up in hell.

"I don't believe in hell," you say. Jesus did, and I'm not going to second-guess Him. Sin is real and the stakes are high.

I wonder why God saw to it that the sorrowful story of Abner was preserved in the Bible. Could it be that it is there to remind you and me that we must not believe false messengers and trust sworn enemies? Could it be that God kept Abner in the Book so that we would see that failing to take action to move toward God is as fatal as Abner's failure to defend himself, run away, or step inside the city of refuge?

There is one positive thing to learn from Abner. Notice that although he had listened to a false messenger, trusted his sworn enemy, and had done nothing to defend himself or remove himself from the area, that right up to the last moment, salvation was available. He could have stepped into the city of refuge.

It reminds me of the time when Judas betrayed Jesus in the garden by pointing Him out with a kiss of greeting. Judas had sold out, he had collected his money, he had plotted to betray his Lord. But even in the very act of betrayal, Jesus addressed him as "friend." Literally, the word He used to Judas means "Friend of my heart." "Friend of My heart, why have you come?" Jesus asked, "Why are you doing this?" As with Abner, so with Judas—right up to the last possible second, mercy was offered. "Friend of My heart, why . . . ?"

That is the question Jesus asks you this morning. You may have listened to some false messengers and yielded to grievous sin. You may have trusted a sworn enemy that has devastated you. You may have failed to take action to give up your sins and step into the ark of safety. You may, right up to this moment, be engaged in acts that can only be described as betraying Christ. But even if all that is true in your case, listen carefully for the still small voice of the Savior, calling you to come to Him, calling you, "Friend of My heart."

You need not die like foolish Abner. The Savior of the world offers you life eternal. Hear His call, "Friend of My heart, come."

||||||||||||||||||||||||||||||||||||||||||

Mary, Lead Us Back to Bethlehem

"Mary, how could you risk everything that matters in life?"

TEXT: Luke 1:26-56

It happened on a Wednesday. In Galilee, a very long time ago, on some ordinary and unknown Wednesday, Joseph and his family representatives met with the family representatives of a young girl named Merium—Mary to us. At that meeting, a betrothal contract was signed. Such contracts for maidens, virgins if you please, were always drawn up on Wednesdays. Betrothal contracts for widows became business for Thursdays. For young Mary, everything seemed so set, so final, so right, now that the contract was signed.

Mary and Joseph—very common names, particularly Mary. Every family, it seems, had a Merium named after Moses' sister. Girls were not named after their fathers and grandfathers; that honor was reserved for sons. In fact, many girls were not named at all until they were several years old. Indeed, it was common for a family to have more than one girl named Mary. Mary the elder and Mary the younger, they were usually called. And so it was, that on an ordinary Wednesday long, long ago, an utterly ordinary Mary was betrothed to an ordinary Joseph.

Joseph himself was no scholar. He was not a rabbi. He had no college degree, no B.A., M.A., or Ph.D. No, Joseph was the industrial arts type—a carpenter. He and utterly ordinary Mary, who looked like a hundred other nearly nameless, dark-eyed, olive-complexioned Marys, were betrothed in a little backwoods town called Nazareth.

An Amazing Announcement

Perhaps Mary would have been perfectly happy to have been an ordinary Jewish wife and mother. But God interrupted this idyllic scene. He sent His angel Gabriel with an amazing announcement. The angel said to Mary:

"Behold, you will conceive in your womb and bear a son, and you shall call his name Jesus.

"He will be great, and will be called the Son of the Most High; and the Lord God will give to him the throne of his father David, and he will reign over the house of Jacob for ever; and of his kingdom there will be no end."

And Mary said to the angel, "How shall this be, since I have no husband?"

And the angel said to her, "The Holy Spirit will come upon you, and the power of the Most High will overshadow you; therefore the child to be born will be called holy, the Son of God. . . . For with God nothing will be impossible" (Luke 1:31-35, 37).

This message is amazing because of the nature of it. Just when we begin to learn enough about God's system of nature to understand its reliability, God, in the central event of all history, decides to supersede it. He proclaims an amazing announcement that no law of physics can explain, that no scientist can hypothesize, that no computer can predict. Quite beyond the boundaries of biology, God announces that the Son of the Most High will be born of a virgin!

It is an announcement so amazing, so supranatural, and so suprarational, that ever since, people, especially theologians, have been scurrying about trying to ferret out a natural explanation for it all. For we, especially the theologians, can no more tolerate something suprarational than we can tolerate a roach in our soup.

An Amazing Assignment

It was an amazing announcement, but it was also an amazing assignment. How amazing that God chose utterly ordinary Mary. But it is not just her ordinariness that makes her a risky choice. Consider, for example, Mary's age—she is a 14-year-old child. How in the world can God trust such an important role in cosmic redemption to a 14-year-old? Jewish girls were usually betrothed at about age 12 but not given in marriage until full puberty—about age 15. It was somewhere between betrothal and being given in marriage that the Virgin Mary was "found to be with child" (Matt. 1:18). And so we will think of Mary as a 14-year-old.

You know what 14-year-old girls are like—they are giggly junior highers, they freak out over rock and roll singers, they are boy-crazy, they wear T-shirts with absurd sayings on them. Immaturity of the rankest sort!

It looks like God could have found a devout, virginal type of woman of 35 or so. Sarah was nearly 100 when she gave birth, wasn't she? Mary was a high risk and an amazing choice. She could hardly have worked her way through her teenage identity crisis yet.

An Amazing Acceptance

It was indeed an amazing announcement and an amazing assignment, but even more astonishing was Mary's amazing acceptance.

At first, Mary was "greatly troubled at the saying, and considered in her mind" what all this meant (v. 29). Wouldn't you be "greatly troubled" and do some considering as well?

Mary was greatly troubled, but, considering it seriously, she responded with these amazing words: "Let it be to me according to your word" (v. 38). Just what did Mary put to risk in order to obey God?

First, she certainly risked family rejection and disapproval. She would have to bear the burden of bringing disgrace to the family. What would her brothers and sisters say? What would her parents think? Oh, you say, surely her parents would understand—they would believe her story. Perhaps, but they would believe her to about the same degree that you would believe your 14-year-old who turned up with a story like Mary's.

Further, Mary risked *public disapproval*. In saying, "Let it be to me according to your word," she was accepting the assignment to be gossip bait in a small town. Notice the wording of Matt. 1:18, "she was found to be with child." She agreed to the risks of being pregnant out of wedlock when that brought the bitterest sort of despising.

Scholem Asch, in his historical novel, *Mary,* says that the traditional wedding ceremony included the requirement for the bride to sit in front of her father's house for parts of three days. She was to have her hair loosed, and she was to be dressed in white to signify her virginity. There she sat to receive greetings and good wishes from one and all. But Mary was found to be with child, or as they would have said in those days, she already had a baby beneath her heart.

Do you suppose Mary went through with this? What kinds of greetings from passersby would a pregnant girl dressed in bridal white receive? If you were the parents, would you allow your pregnant teenager to sit as a spectacle before all, and pregnant, protest that she was pure? But that was the kind of risk that the troubled young Mary agreed to when she said, "Let it be to me according to your word." What an amazing acceptance!

But there was more risk. Surely, as far as she knew, when Mary accepted this amazing assignment, she was *saying a final good-bye to her fiancé.* There goes her chance for love and marriage and family. Surely, the just man Joseph would have nothing to do with her now. He could never understand. Would he not now cast her out like a loathsome leper?

There was this too—if her faith turned out to be fevered fantasy, *with Joseph went her means of economic support.* Wife and mother was about the only vocation offered in those days to utterly ordinary Marys. Who would want her and her "illegitimate" child now?

But Mary's amazing acceptance meant *a still greater risk than all this.* Jewish law provided that a betrothed maiden being discovered to be with child by a third person was to be stoned to death. If she was a priest's daughter, she was to be burned to death. However, in later times, this had been mitigated to mere death by strangulation. But, being willing to risk her very life to serve God, Mary answered, "Let it be to me according to your word."

In short, Mary jeopardized everything that really matters—family, reputation, love and marriage, financial security, and her own mortal life—in order to serve God.

Can you think of a better example of complete consecration to God?

The Bible gives us the story of Mary so that we can see what self-surrender and self-denial look like.

By listening to Mary say, "Be it unto me according to thy word" (KJV), we learn that self-surrender is

more than giving up chocolate for Lent . . .

more than feeling sanctimonious about making do with last year's Easter dress . . .

more than cutting down on the time you waste watching frivolous television programs

Meister Eckhart said that "half-Christians" will give up *possessions* and *friends,* and even sacrifice *honors,* but they still fail, he says, to "disown themselves."

Self-surrender has to do with abandoning our old loyalties and yielding completely to God and good. The old loyalty is our "drum major instinct," or as Adler describes it, our hunger for recognition. Our life, that is, our behavior, is the lung by which our loyalties breathe. Self-denial means surrender to God at the level of the very essence of our existence. It means giving over the nerve center of our very being to God. It is scary, and painful. Paul describes it as a "crucifixion."

But it is a joyous liberation too. Hannah Whitall Smith urges, "Be glad and eager to throw yourself headlong into His dear arms. . . . Give up everything that is separate from Him."

For Mary, self-surrender took the form of agreeing to risk and abandoning, if necessary, everything that really mattered. She did not have to accept the assignment. When the angel started talking about things that would wreck her reputation, she could have said, "Hold it right there. The Scriptures say that 'a good name is rather to be chosen than great riches' [Prov. 22:1, KJV]. And the one thing I've got that's worth more than money is my reputation. Sorry, you are asking too much." But instead she said, "Be it unto me according to thy word."

When Gabriel brought up aspects of the assignment that put to risk Mary's marriage, she could have retorted, "You want me to go through divorce and disgrace. Not me, pal. Joseph is my chance for love and happiness—I'm not giving him up for anything!"

When Gabriel began to speak of things that could put an end to her economic security, Mary could have responded like this. "Look, I've got my life planned. I'm marrying a good man with a good trade. He's not rich, but he's got a decent job. We're going to have a nice, suburban, three-bedroom ranch and raise kids. I'm going to join the PTA, cook lasagna for the church suppers, sing in the choir, take the kids to piano lessons in the station wagon, and cheer for the Nazareth High football team. In other words, I've got a nice, quiet life planned. I don't want anyone to mess it up."

But, of course, Mary said, "Be it unto me according to thy word."

An Amazing Adoration

Mary heard an amazing announcement, accepted an amazing assignment, and, because of this, she participated in an amazing adoration.

Some Christians truly adore Mary. Most Protestants don't. Some do not even know how it came to be that her name is associated with a desperate fling of the pigskin in the waning seconds of the football game. Some do not even know why the "immaculate reception" is a clever, though nearly sacrilegious, football phrase.

But in this part of the sermon I am not primarily concerned about the adoration that Mary received, but rather the amazing adoration of the Babe that Mary witnessed and pondered in her heart.

We observe who came to adore the Babe. The shepherds, some Gentile foreigners (the wise men we call them), and two senior citizens at church, Simeon and Anna. And as we join Mary in pondering this in our hearts, we learn that *Divinity is always discovered by those who seem least likely to find it.*

Where were the princes and kings, the rich and the noble—those important enough to greet the newborn King? Where were the high priests, the scribes, the prophets, and the Pharisees—those religious professionals who should have known enough to greet the Babe?

Fulton Sheen wrote:

> Only two classes of people found the Babe: the shepherds and the Wise Men; the simple and the learned; those who knew that they knew nothing, and those who knew that they did not know everything. He is never seen by the arrogant; never by the man who thinks he knows. Not even God can tell the proud anything! Only the humble can find God! (*The Life of Christ*, p. 55).

As we ponder this amazing adoration with Mary, we also learn that *Divinity is always where you least expect to find it.*

A donkey stall, a stable, the filthiest place in the world—here Purity is born. No worldly mind would ever expect to find Divinity there. And to paraphrase Fulton Sheen again, no worldly mind would ever have suspected that He, from whose hands came planets and worlds, would one day have tiny baby hands, that He, whose feet trod the everlasting hills, would one day be too weak to walk, that He, the Eternal Word, would one day be unable to speak even one word.

No worldly mind would ever have suspected that omnipotence would be wrapped in swaddling clothes, that salvation would lie in a manger, that the bird who built the nest would be hatched therein.

No one would ever have suspected that God, breaking in upon human history, would ever be so helpless, and that is precisely why so many miss Him—Divinity is always where you least expect to find it (Sheen, pp. 55-56).

Amazing, is it not? Paul M. Bassett, in his book of Christmas sermons, *Keep the Wonder*, cites Martin Luther's amazement at it all. Luther marvels that God came to us as a mere mewling, a puking Baby.

As we ponder all of this with Mary, we begin to get a clue about the way God does things. *God's way is not the way of the rich and famous*—not the way of kings, and presidents, and armies, military parades, ICBMs, arms dealers, and secret police. God's way is not the way of the influence peddlers and the power brokers. Rather, God's way is about loving, self-sacrificing vulnerability! The Son of the Most High came as a helpless, defenseless Baby. As Rob Staples says, it was an "utterly incomprehensible condescension" fueled by love and vulnerability.

You do understand that if Jesus came into this generation, He could not make His entrance on Malcolm Forbes' $450 million yacht, don't you, even if Malcolm were still alive to throw a party for Him?

You do see how much more fitting it was to invite the shepherds—who were watching the Temple *flocks, animals destined for sacrifice*—how much more fitting to send *them* to see the *real Lamb of God*. You do see that human "pomp and circumstance" are mere nonsense syllables to God.

Another thing we learn as we ponder with Mary is that *the real Christmas story is unswervingly subversive to a sinful world order*. The Christmas story will sink Mr. Forbes' yacht. Listen to Mary ponder these things in her "Song" in Luke 1:46-56. She prophetically proclaims that in Christ we see that God has "scattered the proud" and "put down the mighty," and "the rich he has sent empty away." Paul ponders this, too, and says, "God chose what is foolish in the world to shame the wise, God chose what is weak in the world to shame the strong, God chose what is low and despised in the world, even things that are not, to bring to nothing things that are" (1 Cor. 1:27-28).

The rich, powerful, oppressive establishment will be brought down, and the weak, the poor, the lowly, and the least likely will be exalted. The very foundations of sinful human society are threatened by the Christmas story. The gospel of Christmas is diametrically opposed to the methods and purposes of the military-industrial complex that runs this world. The Christmas reality calls into question the very foundations, the very *givens* of this age.

If, when, and to the extent that the church as an institution models herself after the example of kings and armies, military parades, executive orders and secret police, influence and power brokers of the world—if, when, and to the extent that it does this, it will find the gospel of Christmas unswervingly subversive to the church herself. The power brokers and self-seekers in the church will be assuredly toppled, not by carnal, worldly weapons, but by humble, self-sacrificing, poured-out *vulnerability*. The terrible meek will get them.

Some preachers, impatient with a helpless Baby of a Messiah, will remind us, "Remember, Jesus will grow up and make demands." But that is to miss the point! Just by being a *Baby*, He makes the strongest kind of demand on us already. If you do not know that the Christmas gospel is subversive, you have not yet really heard the Christmas story. You know what the trouble is with Charles Dickens' famous story, *A Christmas Carol?* The trouble is that after Tiny Tim cries out, "God bless us every one," the very next day Bob Cratchet and his neighbors have to go back to work in a sweatshop!

The big threat to Christmas is not Rudolph the Red-Nosed Reindeer, Santa Claus, or the commercializing that goes on at J. C. Penney's. The big threat to Christmas is preachers who won't tell the subversive truth about Christmas—and laity who love to have it so, who think that if the poignant little stories make them cry, they have really had a great Christmas!

But the gospel of Christmas is more than social commentary. It deals with personal salvation as well. And as we ponder with Mary, we see what Mary surely says: Life takes on meaning primarily because of and in relationship to the Babe of Bethlehem. Without Christ, neither you and I nor Mary would matter much.

Ponder this too. You have not yet really heard the

Christmas story if you do not see in the Babe of Bethlehem God's ultimate response to your rebellious and wicked sins. Look at the Babe in the manger and ponder this: That little, vulnerable Baby is what God finally decided to do about you, a sinner.

||||||||||||||||||||||||||||||||||||||||||||||

What One Mother Did for Her Delinquent Daughter

Do not be surprised when you discover that the things you once loved no longer satisfy, that you can no longer enjoy sin.

SCRIPTURE LESSON: Matt. 15:21-28; Mark 7:24-30

Ten times in Jesus' three-year ministry He went on a vacation, or a retreat. That is, He withdrew from the demands of public ministry for rest, meditation, reflection, and prayer. The event described in our text transpired during one of those retreats.

At this time, Jesus apparently really needed some "down" time to rest and recuperate. Not only did He slip away for a quiet retreat with only His disciples, but this time He went into a foreign country in an effort to escape the crowds of people who had depleted His spiritual energies with their needs and demands. He "departed into the coasts of Tyre and Sidon" (Matt. 15:21, KJV). He checked in at the local Holiday Inn or the Super 8 (I can't see Jesus at the Hilton). The Bible actually says that He "entered a house, and would not have any one know it" (Mark 7:24).

But it wasn't long before someone found out that Jesus of Nazareth was in town. Can you ever trust a hotel clerk? Or maybe a talkative maid noticed the name on the housekeeping list. Perhaps something like this happened. Jesus is just a dozen minutes into a nap on the king-sized bed. Then comes a knock on the door, gently at first, then harder, then urgent. Knowing that no one had called out for pizza or called room service for club sandwiches and Cokes, the disciples smelled a rude interruption. Peter, or James, or John peers carefully out through the drawn drapes. "It's just some hysterical Canaanite woman; Syrophenician, I'd say, by the way she's dressed. Ignore her; she will go away."

Later, Jesus and His disciples appear in the street, and they discover that she has not gone away, and that she will not go away. She cries out, "O Lord, thou Son of David." That's just what they need, right? A public announcement of who Jesus is—this is one quiet retreat that is about to go down the drain. The disciples, shielding Jesus like a bunch of Secret Service agents protecting the president, try to walk away from her. But she cries after them, "Have mercy on me." They try to push her away. "Get lost, lady," they tell her. But desperately, her voice raspy and hoarse by now, she pushes her way through them and throws herself at Jesus' feet. "My daughter is grievously vexed with a devil" (KJV), she sobs. Or to paraphrase, "My daughter is literally possessed by a demon." Or, as we might say it today, "My daughter is full of the devil, and I don't know what to do." What did she mean by that? I'm not sure, but I like the way Joe W. Burton suggests that she is crying out, "My daughter has thrown off all moral restraint."*

Look at this woman. Has she no pride? No dignity? Here she is, making a scene in public. Begging, crying, pleading, right here on Main Street. Has she no concern for manners, for the appropriate way of getting counseling? And so loud, the Bible says she was "shrieking" after Jesus. What a pathetic creature, a quivering mass of pain, humiliation, grief, tears, and begging.

And what did Jesus do about it? At first, He just ignored her—He "answered her not a word" (Matt. 15:23, KJV). Then, when He did speak, He told her that He did not come into this world to minister to Gentile dogs like her and her daughter (Matt. 15:26). But on she pleaded, "Lord, help me." Had she lost all self-respect? He called her and her daughter "dogs," but she ignored the insult and kept on praying, "Lord, help me . . . my daughter is full of the devil."

What a pitiful sight. Parents whose children are full of the devil do strange things. They forget about "nice and proper" and go straight to "heartbroken and desperate."

That's where this Canaanite woman was. She did not care about appearances, she cared about a daughter who had so thrown off moral restraints that it was obvious she was filled with the devil. What a pathetic creature.

And let me say to the young people here today, that you have the power to make your parents look exactly like this Canaanite woman. You can bring them to their knees. Are they too proud, too high and mighty anyway—you can change all that. You can change almost any parent into a quivering mass of tears and grief and pain and sorrow. You can, as they say, put those parents through the meat grinder. You can yank them through a knothole. You can make them say, "I didn't know I could hurt this bad."

How? Just act like the girl in our text today. Throw off moral restraints. Let the devil have his way with you. Make sin your "good." Eagerly pursue every lustful temptation. Neglect no chance to embrace wickedness.

Fry your brain on drugs.

Have sex with anyone and everyone (AIDS and herpes is what other people get).

Become the most regular customer at the local abortion clinic.

Sell marijuana on campus; snort coke in your room.

Flunk out of school.

Get jailed for DWI. (Let your parents spend a few thousand bailing you out and hiring you a lawyer.)

Yes, you can bring them to their knees. There are dozens of possibilities. With just a little effort, you can bring them to the point where life is not worth living. Parents are amazingly impressionable, so it's easy to beat up on them psychologically. Tell them that you hate them. Tell them that they never loved you. Tell them that your addiction to alcohol, drugs, or lust is their fault—they will believe you! You see, they would rather blame themselves than you.

So you don't think your mom and dad pray enough—you can change that in a hurry. Just start living like you are full of the devil. They will be on their knees in no time. You can check to see if it's working. Listen carefully in the middle of the night by their private door. Chances are you will hear one or both of them moaning and groaning and weeping, begging God to save you before you go too far and ruin your life and hurt too many people. You have them where you want them. They are in the palm of your hand. You have a chain in their noses. You couldn't make them beg any more if you held a .357 Magnum to their temples.

Did your parents fail to give you enough attention? Well, start giving yourself boldly and brazenly to sin, and you will get their attention, and lots of it. In fact, they will soon come to the place where nothing else matters but you.

Your parents too religious? Maybe you can get them to lose their faith and throw it in the trash like a worn-out sock. You see, they have invested a lot in you. They sent you to Sunday School, taught you to pray, to pay your tithe. They sent you to VBS, to church camp, to revivals—they bought you a Bible when you were little, and then bought you a *Living Bible* later. But you can prove to them that all those things, and all the other things they did for you, did not work—and maybe they will just give up! Maybe they will quit trying and join that great host of parents disillusioned with religion, a religion that did not work for them. They go muddling along, living their own version of the life of quiet desperation. If you get within a heartbeat of them, you discover a basic sadness, a current of continuous hurt, and only a cautious faith where once a rambunctious faith romped. Like learning to live with a limp, they have adjusted, but not much really matters anymore. You could shove your parents in that direction.

If you are dramatic enough, you may even get the Christian friends of your parents to club them over the head with Prov. 22:6, "Train up a child in the way he should go: and when he is old, he will not depart from it" (KJV). The cruelest thing about this holy "club" is that most of the people who wield it don't understand it. The King James translation is not as clear as it should be. Even the most conservative commentaries point out that this verse is more about vocation than salvation. Educators hail this wise word from Solomon as an educational revolution. Its meaning is, "Train a child in a vocation to which he is suited, and it will be a source of satisfaction to him all his life." Nevertheless, if handled cleverly, the misuse of this scripture can convince your parents that they were terrible at parenting. Maybe they will just quit praying for you and give up in despair. On the other hand, they may be like the Canaanite woman and refuse to stop praying. And, as we shall see later, this could be bad news for you and the devil.

The Severe Testing of One Mother's Prayers

The Canaanite mother's prayer was desperate and urgent. Yet was any mother's prayer ever so severely tested?

First, it was tested by the disdain and impatience of the disciples. Those closest to Jesus did not want to be bothered with this person. She was, after all, a woman and a Gentile. They did not want to bother with her, and they did not want her wasting the time and energy of Jesus. "Stop nagging," they told her. "Get out of here. Stop crying after us. Be quiet and be gone."

Some of you men know how they felt. Nothing rankles a man more than a woman who won't give up but goes on and on and on and never knows when to stop, but just keeps on and won't let an issue drop. So, angrily they said to Jesus, "Send her away. She is crying after us. We can't stand it anymore. Send her away."

Looking back, we can see that the very persons who should have been bringing people to Christ (the disciples) were, by their disdain and their impatience, sending people away from Christ. We know better now, don't we? Those of us in the church would never disdain or send away "undesirables" whose gender or race or social status we find offensive, would we? But that's another subject—thankfully. We are examining the way this mother's prayers were tested. Her prayer was indeed tested by the disciples. The very ones from whom one would expect understanding, sympathy, and love, the very ones whom you would expect to bring this needy soul to the feet of Jesus—they wanted her to shut up and get out of their sight.

Second, her prayer was tested by the silence of the Sav-

ior. When this poor, desperate, distracted woman flung herself in the dust before Him and clutched His feet in supplication, Jesus acted as if He didn't even hear her sobbing prayer, "Lord, help me" (Matt. 15:25, KJV). "He answered her not a word," the Bible says (v. 23, KJV). Have you ever been there? Have you ever flung yourself down at that wellworn spot at the end of your rope and cried out to God from the depths of a broken heart, and the only thing you could hear was the echo of your own voice as your lonely prayers drifted off, unheeded, into space? I remember taking off to pray for a loved one. For three weeks I prayed six hours a day, but as far as I could tell, nothing happened.

I once took my granddaughter Mindy with me to a country church where I was the guest preacher. Before I delivered the sermon, I introduced Mindy to the congregation. That embarrassed her a little, and after church, my four-year-old granddaughter asked me why I did it. "Because I'm proud of you, and because I'm glad you came with me," I said. "That's better than ignoring you," I added. Then, remembering that she was only four years old, I asked, "Do you know what *ignore* means?"

"Yes," she said, "it means to pretend you're not there." Mindy was right, and that's just the way Jesus treated the Canaanite mother who fell at His feet. He pretended, at first, that she was not there. "He answered her not a word." Her prayer was tested by the disdain and impatience of the disciples, and it was tested even more by the silence of the Savior. But the worst was yet to come.

Her prayer was tested by humiliation and insult. When Jesus finally acknowledged the woman's presence and spoke to her, He called her a dog. And He called her daughter a dog. "I am not sent but unto the lost sheep of the house of Israel," He said. And then He added, "It is not meet [right] to take the children's bread, and to cast it to dogs" (KJV).

Right away we ask, why would Jesus be so rude? Why would He treat anyone like that? The question is partially answered when we realize, as most interpreters say, that Jesus' remarks were aimed more at the disciples than the praying woman. Jesus was demonstrating to the disciples

103

how ridiculous their "exclusive" doctrine was. They were infected with the notion that it was Jews that God was out to save—not Gentiles. It was the disciples who believed that Jesus was to minister only to the lost sheep of Israel, not our Lord. He was repeating their prejudice so that they could see how dumb it was. Here was a woman with a desperate need, she had prayed fervently and persistently, and her faith was obvious to all. Jesus is showing His narrow-minded followers how stupid it would be to answer the prayer of such a person by saying, "Sorry, old girl. You're the wrong nationality." Jesus, and later the Holy Spirit, had to teach this lesson to the disciples several times before they caught on (see Acts 10 and 11, and Galatians 2).

The disciples may have thought that Jesus had chosen this particular spot for the retreat because of the king-sized beds, or the new sauna, or maybe the cable TV, but it was much more likely that Jesus chose this spot beyond the boundary of Israel so that He could show the disciples how much God cares for the Gentiles whom they themselves could hardly tolerate.

But all this on-the-job training did not help the poor Canaanite mother. How would she respond to being called a dog? Here's her response: "she . . . worshipped him, saying, Lord, help me" (Matt. 15:25, KJV). Interpreting her actions and words, we see that her response was, "You've called me a dog. You've called my daughter a dog. But that's all right. I refuse to be offended. You can call me anything you like—I am way beyond being hurt or insulted. But, you see, my daughter is full of the devil. Call me anything, but deliver her from the evil one."

Then she picked up Jesus' own metaphor and used it in diminutive form. She changed the term from "dog" to "little dog." "I'm not even a dog," she was saying, "I'm just a little dog. I don't want the whole meal, I just want a crumb. Lord, help me—my daughter is full of the devil." Jesus called her a Gentile dog, and she responded, "Yes, Lord: yet the dogs under the table eat of the children's crumbs" (Mark 7:28, KJV).

It is one thing to have your prayer tested by divine silence. It is quite another when it seems that the Divine One mocks your prayers. Was anyone's prayers more severely tested? She had every reason and plenty of excuses to turn aside and give up. Her prayer was tested by an exclusive doctrine, by sexist prejudice, by the impatience and disdain of the disciples, by her own sense of unworthiness, by the silence of Jesus, and by what seemed like divine mockery of her, her daughter, and her prayer.

And yet, was there ever a prayer that was so wondrously answered? Jesus looked at her and marveled at her faith. In compassion, He said to her, "For such a reply, you may go; the demon has left your daughter." Quickly she ran home "and found her child lying on the bed, and the demon gone" (Mark 7:29-30, NIV).

I do not know what the demon was. Frequently in those times they called any disorder that they could not understand, whether it was psychological, physical, or spiritual, a demon. Whatever it was in this case, we do know that it was a power or force greater than this mother or daughter could handle. There was no pill to take for it, no known cure, no treatment. The victim could only be made whole by divine power. In this case, deliverance came about through persistent prayer and by the power of Jesus Christ.

I know some people in the same predicament, don't you? Some persons who are pushed about by powers greater than themselves? Persons for whom there is no hope except through divine intervention? What are we to do for them? Pray like the Canaanite mother prayed. Pray and never give up. Pray, even when it seems God does not hear, even when it seems He may be mocking you. Pray.

This story in the Bible does not guarantee that if we pray loud enough and long enough that all our children will be saved, but it does give us hope. It teaches us that when it comes to praying for our children, it is always too soon to give up.

One teenage girl I know about ran away from home. For 10 years her mother never got a letter, never once heard the sound of her daughter's voice. But she prayed every day. Then one night, a decade after the daughter ran away, the phone rang, and her daughter asked, "Mama, can I come home?"

Let me address the youth here today. Like I said earlier, you can bring your parents to their knees. You can reduce them to a quivering mass of grief. But it is only fair to warn you about the power of a mother's prayer or a father's prayer. It is only fair to warn you that if your parents pray for you like the Canaanite mother prayed, the Holy Spirit, like the Hound of heaven, may stay on your wayward trail day and night.

Do not be surprised that at every turn in your pursuit of pleasure, money, fun, sexual freedom, you encounter a challenging God. Do not be surprised that, in answer to your parents' prayers and the work of the Holy Spirit, you discover

> that you can no longer enjoy sin
> that illicit pleasures lose their taste
> that the things you once loved no longer satisfy
> that the God-shaped hunger in the center of your soul can no longer be ignored
> and that one of these days, without really knowing why, you will come back to God, broken in spirit and seeking the One who can make you whole again

There is no guarantee that this will happen. No one can be saved against his will. But the story of the Canaanite woman is in our Bible in order for us to learn not to be surprised when God answers prayer and miraculously makes lost children whole again.

*Joe W. Burton, *Home Life* magazine, May 1971, p. 46. The author acknowledges indebtedness to Joe W. Burton for several insights into the interpretation of the passage of scripture treated in this sermon.

| | | | | | | | | | | | | | | | | | | | | | | | | | | | | | | | | | | | | | | |

Luke's Little Brother

Happiness is not something you find, it is something you create in cooperation with God.

Only one Gentile ever wrote anything good enough to make it into the Bible. You have 66 books in the Bible you tucked under your arm as you left for church today. Sixty-four of them were written by Hebrews, 2 by a Gentile. Who was that special Gentile whose two books became scripture? His books are the two longest ones in the New Testament: Luke and Acts. In addition, Luke may have been the secretary to whom Paul dictated some of his letters to the churches that also became holy scripture. This fellow Luke is a Very Important Person, a VIP in the true sense of the word.

Without Luke, we would know very little about the earliest Church. Only through his writings do we learn of the divine announcements foretelling the births of John the Baptist and Jesus. Without Luke, we would know nothing of the inn that had no room in Bethlehem or the angels that sang on Jesus' birth to the shepherds. And we would know nothing of the shepherds' visit to the manger.

Only Luke records the songs of Mary, Zechariah, and Simeon. Luke alone tells of Jesus' presentation in the Temple, and of His visit to the Temple at age 12. Luke alone tells us of Christ's hearing before Herod, of Jesus' prayer on the Cross, asking forgiveness for His murderers, of Jesus assuring the thief on the cross of eternal salvation, of the marvelous Emmaus Road incident. Only through Luke's patient pen do we learn the parables of the good Samaritan, the prodigal son, the rich man and Lazarus, and the publican and the Pharisee at prayer. How impoverished our knowledge of the earliest Church would be without Luke. Truly, Luke was and is a VIP.

Besides all that Luke alone teaches us about the life of Christ, nearly all of what we know about the first 30 years of the Early Church comes from Luke's history—the Book of Acts. By any standard, Luke was and is a VIP.

Luke traveled with Paul to all the exciting places: Jerusalem, Caesarea, Athens, Philippi, and Rome. He shared Paul's greatest adventures—persecutions of every sort, like a shipwreck off Malta and a trial in Rome.

And Luke was faithful through thick and thin—just before Paul's head was chopped off somewhere out on the Appian Way, he wrote, "Only Luke is with me" (2 Tim. 4:11, KJV). So here is Luke—physician, missionary, evangelist, historian, faithful comrade—a VIP in every sense of the word.

But Luke had a little brother. A faithful, hardworking Christian, and a man of no small talent. He was not as famous as his big brother. He seemed to get mostly dirty work assignments. In fact, one wonders whether or not Luke himself respected his little brother's contribution. When Luke wrote his history of the Early Church, the Book of Acts, he did not once mention his brother's name—even though his brother was one of the prime-time players in many of the events Luke wrote about. Or could it be that Luke failed to mention his brother out of family modesty? His brother was, after all, important enough to have one of the books of the Bible addressed to him.

But whether or not Luke thought his brother was significant, Paul thought very highly of him. Once, when the Board of Bishops bellowed at Paul, "Let's see one of those uncircumcised Gentile Christians you've been bragging about. We want to examine him. We want to grill him." Paul said, "OK, here's Luke's little brother. Have at him." Paul knew he could never find a more sturdy example of a Christian than Luke's little brother.

One of the first ministry assignments given to Luke's little brother had to do with a church fuss. Paul had so incensed the believers at Corinth that he did not dare show up there—even though he had planned and promised to show up. So Paul canceled his trip to this seething church whose members were clenching their fists and grinding their teeth at the mention of his name. Instead of facing them, he wrote them a testy, maybe nasty, letter. He called Luke's little brother and told him that he wanted him to go to Corinth, relieve timid Timothy, and read the folks what came to be known as the "severe letter." Further, Paul told him something like this, "Stand up for me, since I'm afraid to go, and tell them to get off my case because . . . because I'm really a nice guy."

The letter was so severe that no sooner had Luke's little brother disappeared into the sunset than Paul began to wish he had not sent it. Paul was so worried about that letter that he could not wait for Luke's little brother to return, so he set out to meet him halfway home. He set out on the Egnatian Way, traveled into Macedonia, and, sure enough, he met Luke's little brother, who was making his way back to Paul with a report.

The report that Luke's little brother delivered in the middle of some dusty highway in Greece was overwhelmingly positive. It must have sounded like a miracle to Paul. Luke's little brother had walked into that den of snarling Christians, shared the severe letter, reasoned with the people, and convinced them that Paul was their friend and a true apostle. The Bible says that when Luke's little brother left Corinth, the Christians there "longed" for Paul, were sorry they had hurt him, were "eager" to take his side, and were "devoted" to him. The Bible adds that not only did they now like Paul, but also they loved Luke's little brother. And Luke's little brother loved them, too, with a warm heart (2 Cor. 7:15).

Where Paul's favorite, Timothy, had utterly failed, Luke's little brother had dramatically succeeded. He had entered what looked like a hopeless situation and had completely redeemed it. And that was a career mistake! Once a district superintendent finds out that you can take a church that is split and fighting and staffed with carnal board members and turn it around, he will send you to one problem church after another. That was to be the fate of Luke's little brother. While Luke was becoming a VIP, his little brother was becoming a troubleshooter.

After Luke's little brother had experienced such great success at Corinth, Paul, a creative district superintendent, came up with Plan B. Once again he called upon Luke's little brother, telling him that since he was so well liked in Corinth, he was sending him back there to do some fundraising. It seems that the Corinth church was way behind on its "budgets." Luke's little brother, flushed with his recent success, went back to his newfound friends with an offering plate in one hand and a stack of pledge cards in the other. But the good believers at Corinth hooted him down and accused him of trying to raise an offering so that he could steal it and split it with Paul.

This apparently was the first career failure for Luke's little brother. He came out of it a sadder and wiser man. Doubtless the experience helped prepare him for even tougher tasks ahead, for Paul continued to send Luke's little brother out on problem-solving missions.

Then came the big assignment, an assignment so tough, so undesirable, that even Luke's little brother begged to get out of it. Paul sent him to Crete. To Crete of all places!

The people on Crete were true Cretans. Their reputation had been so bad for so long that the Greek word for "to lie" or "to cheat" became "to Cretize." One of the seven wise men of Greece, a philosopher, himself a native of Crete, Epimenides by name, wrote of his countrymen, declaring that they were "chronic liars," "wild, evil beasts," "vicious brutes," and "lazy gluttons." Paul, in a letter to Luke's little brother, says that Epimenides was exactly right about the Cretans.

No wonder Luke's little brother could not stand it there. The Cretans seemed to lead the world in uncivilized practices. The literature of the times describes them as insolent, drunken, untrustworthy, and ready to murder anyone for money. One Polybius says that they were given to private quarrels and public feuds. They were, he said, tricky and deceitful traitors who would do anything for money. No deed was too dishonorable for a Cretan—if he could get paid for it. Crete was the original homeland of the Philistines, those pagan brutes who terrorized the people of God throughout Old Testament times. Who would dare even try to evangelize this bunch! Paul thought that Titus, Luke's little brother, would be just the one for this king-sized task. But not even Paul was always right. We look at Paul's letter to Titus in the New Testament, and we get the idea that it was written in response to a letter from Titus asking to be excused from staying in that dreadful place. Harry Emerson Fosdick has tried to reconstruct the letter from Titus that Paul is answering in the Epistle to Titus. He believed it went something like this:

Dear Paul:
This is an awful place. The inhabitants are hopeless, and the poor and struggling Christian movement is only rags and tatters. I am remaining here until you say, "Go," but I can't get away fast enough. For pity's sake don't make me stay here all winter. There isn't a decent chance. Obediently, but unhappily.

Yours,
TITUS

Then Titus gets Paul's answer, the Epistle to Titus in the Bible, which went something like this: "You are right about the Cretans; they are dishonest, drunken, brutal beasts, lazy gluttons—everything you and Epimenides said about them is true. In fact, you could not exaggerate their sinful wickedness. Crete is in deep need." And then came the clincher, the deathknell to Titus' hope of escaping from Crete quickly. I paraphrase Paul: "You are right, Titus, they are rotten sinners [v. 5] and this is why I left you in Crete! I left you in Crete, Titus, because nobody needs the gospel more than those depraved people of Crete."

Paul goes ahead to tell Titus that he knows he will have to deal with people who are "insubordinate," "empty talkers," "deceivers," people who are "ruining whole families" (NIV), who are "teaching for base gain"—and these are the people in the church! Paul goes on (1:15-16). These people have corrupted minds and corrupted consciences. They profess to work for God, but their deeds deny Him. They are in fact "detestable, disobedient, unfit for any good deed." Titus was to "rebuke them sharply" (v. 13). And by the grace of God and the power of the Spirit he was to make of these miscreant Cretans a community of faith (2:1-10) filled with redeemed people who were temperate, serious, sensitive, sensible, reverent, not slanderers, not slaves to drink, chaste, kind, and self-controlled. In short, this raucous crowd was to be transformed into a people who "adorn the doctrine of God our Savior" (2:10). "In other words," Paul was saying, "I left you in Crete, Titus, so that you could turn the nation upside down. From vicious brutes make sensitive saints, turn grabbers into givers, liars into lovers of God."

So, while Luke and Paul were touring the Mediterranean making history, Titus stayed in Crete to make converts.

There he was, stuck in Crete. He had to minister to people with whom he had little in common, in a place he did not like, and under circumstances as unpleasant as a tenement slum. But he got results. During those early times when Christianity was conquering the Roman Empire, a veritable stream of teachers, preachers, and missionaries came out of Crete—thanks to Titus who let Christ use him in an unlikely place.

And if you visit Crete today, your tour guide will show you several magnificent churches. He will point to a brass plaque on each of them and tell you that the plaque says, "In honor of St. Titus." He will show you the tomb of Titus, a shrine really, and he will say to you and your group, "St. Titus was the first to evangelize this island. And he did a good job too, for today 98 percent of the people who live on this island are Christians."

Meditating on the Life of Titus

Perhaps the story of Titus is in our Bible so that we can examine it and draw from it some truths that will help us answer the call of God upon our lives. The life of Titus dramatizes several truths.

1. The Aim of Life Is Not to Compete with, to Outclimb, or to Outperform Your Brother or Sister or Class-

mates or Parents—but to Serve God and Your Fellow Human Beings

For some people the hardest thing for them to bear is the success of a brother or sister. Once, in ancient times, a certain priest withdrew to the desert, joining a monastic community in order to give himself to prayer, solitude, and the search for a pure heart. Satan assigned a rookie demon to harass him. The demon tried everything to defeat the determined holy man. He fixed it so that every time the holy man closed his eyes to pray, he saw visions of the most beautiful dancing girls in Rome. When he opened his eyes, he saw visions of a sumptuous banquet table laden with great platters of roasted beef, broiled fish, and game cooked in the most succulent sauces. Mounds of rare fruits and desserts of every sort also beguiled him. Sparkling wine glistened, and pitchers of the best ale and fountains of spring water tempted this lonely man in the desert. The demon also fixed it so that the only sound the holy man could hear was the clinking of gold coins being poured out upon a table. But nothing worked. Though the demon promised the man gold and feasting and female companionship, the holy man would not give up his dedicated search for a pure heart and union with God.

Satan came along one day to see how the fledgling demon was progressing in his attempt to damn the holy man. The demon reported all that he had done. He hung his head in despair, ready to give up. But Satan said, "Watch this." Whereupon he approached the praying holy man and whispered in his ear, "Your brother has just been made bishop of Alexandria." Immediately an angry scowl covered the face of the holy man, and he rose from prayer almost in a rage. "There," said Satan to his junior cohort, "that is the sort of thing I recommend."

The temptations of the flesh he could overcome—but the success of his brother was simply too much to bear.

Perhaps you have read the story of two brothers who were rabbis. They lived in the same house and served in the same synagogue. They were, it seemed, models of brotherly love. Because of their many years of service, an angel appeared to them one day and informed them that either one of them could make a wish, and whatever was asked for would surely be granted. There was just one condition. The brother who made the wish would be given what he asked for, but the other brother would receive the same thing, only double. The wish had to be made before sundown. You guessed it—they spent the day trying to get each other to make the wish. "What were you thinking of wishing for?" one asked the other. "Well, I was thinking of wishing for a bushel of diamonds, but the thought of your having two bushels is more than I can bear. What would you wish for if you made the wish?" "Well," answered the second brother, "I was thinking of wishing for a roomful of gold, but the idea of your having two rooms full of gold makes me sick. After all, I have been the hard worker in the family. I am the one who has sacrificed most." And so they badgered each other all day long. The sun hung on the horizon, about to disappear in a grape-colored sunset. "Hurry, make a wish," yelled the first brother, "before we lose it all." "I wish," said the other brother at the last possible second, "to be blind in one eye."

Luke's little brother was not the victim of such sibling rivalry. While Luke made history, Titus was content to make converts in an unpleasant situation. How many people today, some of them 50 years old, are still trying to outshine a brother, a sister, or a parent. Titus tells us that the aim of life · is not to compete and win over your brother but to serve wherever God puts you.

The second truth to be drawn from the story of Titus is:

2. You Can Expect God to Call You to Crete
It is just like God to call His children to serve in Crete. We sing

> *Some through the waters,*
> *Some through the flood,*
> *Some through the fire,*
> *But all through the Blood—*

and some sort of Crete, we might add.

Some Cretes to which we are called are of a personal and social nature. There is the Crete of personal disadvantage, of physical handicaps, of mental and intellectual limitations. There is the Crete of "meanness of opportunity," to use George Eliot's phrase. Some have to cope with the Crete of a wrong marriage, or a divorce that they did not want—or a divorce they wanted for all the wrong reasons. Some must cope with career failure, crushing debt, or the long shadow of a disgraceful past.

Some must face the fact that God has called them to serve in out-of-the-way places like Crete. Some must always minister, like Titus, to persons with whom they have little in common, in places where the people are distasteful and unappreciative. We must realize that our world is not a flower garden in which to daydream and spin fantasies. No, Christ calls us to the Crete that is our world. He calls us to Crete with its unpleasant odors, its crude and cruel people, and its hard places. Crete cries out to be converted, to be conquered by Christian love. So, expect a call to Crete.

The third principle that we can draw from the life of Titus is

3. There Is No Use Pretending to Be a Disciple of Jesus if We Are Unwilling to Go to Crete and Stay Put Until and Unless God Sends Us Somewhere Else

It is utterly useless to claim to be a disciple of Jesus but say, I will only serve in pleasant places with pleasant people in pleasant surroundings. You cannot be the Lord's servant and refuse to go to Crete just because it is a tough place to work. Hear the scripture again. Hear Paul as he says to Titus, Crete is a hard place, the Cretans are a bad lot. And that is why I sent you to Crete!

Don't you see, Jesus belongs in Crete! Jesus particularly belongs in Crete! Jesus belongs in Crete, not in spite of the fact that Cretans are liars, vicious brutes, drunken gluttons, but precisely because they are!

Who could need Jesus more? You don't expect that Jesus wants us to ignore the most needy Cretes of our world, do you? Do you think that Jesus wants us to ignore the

Cretes of our ghettos, our central cities, our poverty-stricken neighborhoods? Do you think that people today are deprived because God wants it that way? Do you think that He wants the poor and oppressed of this world to live and die unconfronted with the gospel, unwarned of sin, uninstructed in the things of God? Let's face it—there is no use pretending to be a Christian if you are unwilling to "spend and be spent" for the Crete-dwellers of our times.

Mother Teresa one day totally surrendered her life to Christ. Maxie Dunnam wrote of her, "That was the end of her biography and the beginning of her life." When asked why she would give her life to the people in the slums of Calcutta, she said she did it because of an overwhelming sense of debt.

When John Wesley was counseling Miss March, a gentlewoman, on how to get sanctified, he told her again and again to go to Crete. In one letter he said to her, "Go and see the poor and sick in their own little hovels. Take up your cross, woman." Several months later he writes to her, "I want you to converse more abundantly with the poorest of the people who, if they have not taste, have souls." Wesley goes on in the same letter, "Creep in among these in spite of dirt and a hundred disgusting circumstances, and thus put off the gentlewoman." Less than three weeks later Wesley pushes the same issue again to Miss March. He advises her to "frequently, nay, constantly to visit the poor, the widow, the sick, the fatherless." This she is to do even though such persons "have nothing to recommend them but that they are bought by the blood of Christ." She is to expect a "thousand circumstances" to "shock the delicacy of her nature," but this must not keep her from the blessing to be found in this labor of love.

Others received similar advice from Wesley. Theological student Samuel Furly was told in three different letters to break away from academic pursuits regularly in order to visit the sick. Brian Bury Collins, another theological student, was advised, "You have seen very little of the choicest part of London society: I mean the poor. Go with me to their cellars and garrets, and then you will taste their spirits." Wesley believed that God calls His serious servants to Crete.

Your ministry may not duplicate that of Wesley's time. But not many of us would have to travel far to find poor and sick people suffering away in some personal or social Crete. For example, how many grandfathers and grandmothers will spend today looking out of the window of some nursing home, staring at an empty parking lot, hoping that a certain Chevy or Plymouth will appear?

The fourth principle that we learn from the life of Titus is that

4. None of Us Are Too Good to Go to Crete

You are not too good to go to Crete, are you? Listen to Paul speak to Titus about this matter. In chapter 3, Paul tells Titus to stay in Crete because at one time we were no better than they. "For we ourselves," he says, "were once foolish, disobedient, led astray, slaves to . . . passions and pleasures, passing our days in malice and envy, hated . . . and hating one another" (v. 3). No, if we are honest with ourselves, we must admit that we are not too good to go to Crete.

Principle number 5 that we discover in the study of the life of Titus is:

5. Happiness and Fulfillment Depend More on the Person than the Circumstances

After Titus had worked for a few years in Crete, Paul was executed. Titus was his own boss now. He could go anywhere he wanted now. And he decided to stay, to stay in Crete. There he worked with those obnoxious folk until he died at age 93. He was buried in honor. Titus, looking back, would probably say, "I wouldn't change a thing." Titus teaches us that happiness is not something you find, it is something you and the Lord create.

All of life should be tackled the way Titus tackled Crete. Tackle the difficulties in your life the way Titus tackled Crete, and you will discover that you and God make a great team. You will discover that happiness and fulfillment can be made from the most woeful raw materials when you obey God. Seize life by the ears and try.

6. Your Greatest Achievements and Contributions Will Probably Come from Your Sojourn in Crete

Take Paul Lawrence Dunbar, for example. He was trapped like a caged bird by the most vicious kind of racial prejudice. What chance did a Negro writer have in 1900? But caged or not, he rose above cruel discrimination to write some of the greatest poems of his generation, including this one that nearly every American has to read before they let them out of high school.

SYMPATHY

I know what the caged bird feels, alas!
When the sun is bright on the upland slopes
When the wind stirs soft through the springing grass,
And the river flows like a stream of glass:
When the first bird sings and the first bud opens,
And the faint perfume from its chalice steals—
I know what the caged bird feels!

I know why the caged bird beats his wing
Till its blood is red on the cruel bars;
For he must fly back to his perch and cling
When he fain would be on the bough a-swing;
And a pain still throbs in the old, old scars
And they pulse again with a keener sting—
I know why he beats his wing!

I know why the caged bird sings, ah me,
When his wing is bruised and his bosom sore,—
When he beats his bars and he would be free;
It is not a carol of joy or glee,
But a prayer that he sends from his heart's deep core,
But a plea that upward to heaven he flings—
I know why the caged bird sings!

Even a caged bird can sing. Even a Christian in Crete can sing—maybe not in spite of Crete, but because of it.

I read of a woman in England whose Crete came to her in the loss of both arms and both legs. Confined to a hospital room, what could she do? First, she learned to write with her shoulder, using a special apparatus that held a pen. She read the newspaper daily. And she wrote letters. She wrote to people in trouble about whom she read in the papers. She wrote to people in prison, victims of crimes, earthquakes, etc. She would say, "I read of your trouble. I, too, have known trouble. I have found help, even triumph, in Jesus Christ. Let me tell you about Him. . . ."

When this lady died, they found in her files letters from 1,500 persons who had either found Christ or had looked to Him for help in their time of deep trouble. What a ministry for a person with no hands, arms, feet, or legs.

Recently I read of the experience of a Belgian woman during World War II. Her husband was killed in the war. She was pregnant when he died. A few months later an accident during childbirth left her paralyzed. They hoped that with time she would get better, but she got worse. She could not move a limb or a muscle. The only movement she could make was to blink her eyes. But she wanted to be a writer. She really wanted to be a writer. But how do you write when the only act you can perform is to blink?

There is one way. You could have someone recite the letters in the alphabet, and when they got to the letter you wanted next, you could blink. The nuns who worked in the hospital recited the alphabet, and when she blinked, they wrote down the letter she wanted next. She lived for seven years in this state and wrote two books of children's stories and a book of poems. Imprisoned in Crete, the Crete of a body that would not work, that caged bird learned to sing. I wish I could read her songs—those poems she wrote. I'd guess they sound like the song of the soul set free.

I do not tell you stories like these to shame you or to trivialize your problems. No, I tell them to you in order to make your own personal "Crete" seem more conquerable. I'm sure it is God's will to make you victorious in Crete.

Crete is a hard place, the Cretans are a bad lot—but maybe, just maybe, that is why God has sent you there. Overcome the adversities of Crete with the gospel in the power of Christ. It took Luke's little brother a lifetime, but he did it. So can you.